To John
w/ Love

Cliff Preston
&
The Echo

Love is the.
Only answer
regardless the question

CLIFF PRESTON
CHANNELS THE ECHO

CLIFF PRESTON
CHANNELS THE ECHO

Book 1

Answers for thousands
in their journeys
through life

Patrick Kehoe

Printed and bound in Canada.
First Printing September 2004
Second Printing July 2006

Contact:
Cliff Preston   cpreston@becon.org
Patrick Kehoe   pk3@canada.com

Acknowledgment

The transcript of "Psychism for beginners" appeared in
Metapsychology   The Journal of Discarnate Intelligence
Vol 1 #4   Winter 1985/86

The transcript of "Spirituality? The Inside Story" appeared in
Metapsychology   The Journal of Discarnate Intelligence
Vol 3 #4   Winter 1987/88

Cover design by Patrick Kehoe

CONTENTS

Introduction

1. Cliff and Linda Preston

2. The Echo
Original transcripts of channeling sessions   87

Introduction

Cliff Preston began channeling The Echo, a group of timeless, discarnate entities, in the late 1970s to fulfill a need to help others with life's problems.

CLIFF PRESTON CHANNELS THE ECHO Book 1 (2004) introduces readers to the remarkable life and work of Cliff Preston, internationally known channeler of discarnate entities. It shows how Cliff; Linda, his wife and trance director; and The Echo, a nearly uncountable group of spirits, started on a course which brings spiritual wisdom to life's problems.

The first part of the book describes Cliff's difficult life-long personal search for answers to his questions about life and his place in it. It explains his breakthrough with Spirit which has helped thousands of persons who have had contact with him. There is also a moving look into a man's soul as he struggles to help his dying wife recover from illness. This chapter from Cliff's personal diary details Linda's miraculous recovery from encephalitis, after doctors had given up hope. Cliff's own courageous words credit her recovery to the constant attention of alternative practitioners.

The second part of the book presents several exclusive transcripts of Cliff's deep-trance channeling sessions of The Echo. There are two sessions in the presence of the Mitchell-Hedges Crystal Skull, believed to be a 100,000-year-old interplanetary communication device. Other subjects include spirituality, psychism for beginners, meditation and relaxation, imagination - creating your reality, and alcoholism.

Book 2 (2006) portrays the dangers of Cliff's life at sea, more psychic experiences of Canada's ordinary extraordinary psychic couple in many parts of North America, the relationship between Cliff, Linda, and The Echo, and their view of life. There are more transcripts of Cliff's deep-trance channeling sessions of The Echo on such subjects as The Echo, God, the past and future of humanity, and personal dream interpretation.

Book 3   (2008) reveals underwater recovery diving in Cliff's reminiscences, more about their view of life, and more psychic experiences such as   Linda's encounter with Jesus. There are more transcripts of Cliff's deep-trance channeling sessions of The Echo on such subjects as   messages from The Echo, Jesus Christ, Extra-Terrestrials and other mysteries.

I heard about Cliff when I was looking for a trance channeler in the style of Edgar Cayce. Seeing him   channel The Echo was fascinating. He maintained a trance with a new persona and voice for one hour and 29 minutes, never opening his eyes or losing   the mood. His body moved only if his trance director requested the new   persona move it for him. The channeled answers to my questions carried the essence of truth and   went beyond what I had expected. A new world opened.

A short time later, I attended a psychic information and meditation evening. Each guest gave a brief personal introduction. I said that I am a writer and perhaps I will write a book about Cliff Preston and The Echo some day. I said it with some hope, but no conviction.

As I was writing the first book in June, 2004, I asked The Echo during one channeling session, how I had received the definite idea to write and publish a book, a few years after that psychic evening.

The Echo replied:

"This be gentle nudge by we. We wish the informations that be available here to be made known to, that refer, general public. The form of the one Clifford originally wrote its adventures for the purpose of informing its sons about its life as it find   estrangement with sons. However, we wish this be carried an step or two further and allow these informations be shared with all."

I consider Cliff and The Echo my co-authors. They had the idea of a book first. Cliff readily agreed to work together. He provided what he had written previously - the section from his personal diary and passages for what he thought could be an autobiography some day. He provided selected written transcripts of his deep-trance channeling sessions of The Echo. Cliff and Linda answered my questions and approved my suggestions, writing, rewriting, editing, and cover design.

Chapter 1   The Psychic Fair

It was March, 1975. Cliff Preston, a 38-year-old shift-supervisor at a factory in Buffalo, New York, went to a psychic fair with a friend, as a joke, "to watch the weirdoes." This day he would begin to change his own life and eventually the lives of several thousand others.

Cliff was an angry, frustrated man. Raised in poverty and driven by an inner sense that he was different from other people, he had never long fit anywhere. Constantly discouraged that no one took his questions seriously as a child, he had little faith in adults. He had also suffered the stammerer's private hell since soon after the premature death of his alcoholic father when Cliff was seven. The occasional charity of well-meaning neighbors came at a terrible cost - the public ridicule of the boys whose hand-me-down clothing he wore. He was goaded into many childhood fights. The vicious circle would begin with Cliff's difficulty in getting his words out. As he became more self-conscious about this difficulty, the other boys would cut him with cruel words. This increased his inability to get the words out and his reluctance even to try. The taunts would increase until Cliff's outraged sense of justice started fists flying.

His mother's remarriage after two years had brought a new conflict into Cliff's troubled life. He had viewed himself as the new man of his family, even adding to his family's income by selling fruit at his young years. He was now unable to accept a substitute father. He withdrew into his private world, often spending hours alone at play in the woods near his home. In Grade 10, on a day he was an appointed military cadet squad-leader, he raised his rifle-butt into a taunting classmate's jaw,

7

separating several teeth from the fractured bone. His indefinite expulsion from school led to a laborer's job in a local tannery, after he had refused to visit his tormentor's home and apologize to the boy and his parents. The following September, he had returned to school to complete Grade 10. Cliff then turned his back on formal education and worked in a bakery for two years.

After his 18th birthday, he had traded home in Aurora, a town north of Toronto, for the Royal Canadian Navy. He was going to defend his country and find answers by seeing the world. Instead, he had found more difficulties and more disappointments. The answers would be a long time coming.

On this day in 1975, one failed marriage was behind him. Unknown to him, he was nearing the end of his second bad marriage. The shock of it would drive him to his knees. This would be another double-cross from life.

So here he was in Niagara Falls, New York, at his first psychic fair, with a mixture of scorn, curiosity, and hope that finally he may get some answers about life. Was he disappointed or reassured that the psychic practitioners looked like ordinary people? The ones he spoke with seemed intelligent and articulate. "Thinkers", Cliff considered them. He was surprised to find this kind of person at what he anticipated would be a "carnival." They were people who were themselves learning, as well as teaching others to follow the beat of their own drums. They were down-to-earth. They were practical. Even a young couple calling themselves the Alpha State Mind Trainers had their feet firmly on the ground.

Cliff was intrigued. All day, he went from booth to booth engaging these ordinary people in conversation about the questions which had stayed with him all his life. What is the purpose of life? Is there a God? What is a human being's place in the cosmos? Does it matter what kind of lives we lead? Is someone going to judge us?

For the most part, he noticed that the psychics seemed to have a burning desire to help other persons in whatever way they could. He believed that these people were not like some persons, whom he had encountered. Those persons pretended to be moral on Sundays, but acted the opposite during the rest of the week.

8

The psychics seemed to think it was important to deal directly with troubled individuals as helpfully as they could.

The atmosphere of love and the absence of judgmentalism was refreshing. These psychics had a kindly manner which seemed genuine. The skeptic was curious about whether anyone could help him. Still of mixed emotions, Cliff decided to have a reading. He approached a cordoned area of 10 or so tables, each with a psychic reader. For five dollars he could choose the type of reading which appealed to him most from such things as tarot cards, clairvoyance and other things that seemed to offer their own possibilities.

He chose a bearded, older man in a conservative gray suit who claimed to be a clairvoyant from Rochester, N.Y. As his turn came, Cliff sat in front of the softly spoken man who held the attention of a short line of persons. He still feared that listening to a stranger pretend to give him messages from spirits about his life and his family members would be laughable nonsense.

Cliff's reading started poorly. Most of the things the reader told him seemed to make little sense, or none at all. He seemed to be talking about someone else. As Cliff was deciding to tell the reader that he was not talking about Cliff's life, a woman leaned over the rope barrier and startled Cliff with her comment to the reader.

"Excuse me," she said. "I think you are reading about my family and friends."

What was happening here?

The reader turned away from Cliff and spoke to the woman for a minute.

Then he turned back to Cliff and explained that he had been having difficulty seeing into Cliff's life, but had no difficulty seeing through Cliff to others who were standing around.

The reason was that Cliff "was a natural medium, or channel, wide open to the energies of others."

Cliff heard only meaningless words.

"What a crock," he thought. "Just an excuse for his inability to read me."

9

The woman was pleased to receive the information. However, Cliff left the psychic fair confused and disappointed. It would be more than a year before he realized the full truth of the clairvoyant's comment that he is a natural medium. The clairvoyant had predicted how Cliff would recover his life.

***

Ernest Edward Preston and Hazel Preston, a God-fearing, working-class couple in Aurora, had their first daughter, Marion, in 1927. They lost her to complications from scarlet fever and diptheria in 1936. Their second daughter, Fern Louise, was born in 1931. Their only son, Clifford Edward, was born in 1936.

Cliff remembers that Sundays were quiet with church and Sunday school in the morning and visits with friends or family in the afternoon. When his mother took the children to church, they were sent to the church basement, partway through the service, to learn lessons about the Bible. On the occasions that his mother decided not to go to church, he and his sister were still told to go to Sunday school.

When Cliff had foreknowledge that they would be sent on their own, he would hide his play clothing in a small cluster of trees behind a nearby hill. Dressed for Sunday school, he would wave goodbye and run over the hill on his way to the church. When he was out of sight, he changed his clothes and headed for the woods, where he happily remained for the rest of the day.

He started getting into trouble by asking adults the wrong questions. When Cliff was 10, the class was encouraged to ask questions by the Sunday school superintendent, who was piously teaching about Adam and Eve, as if they were real people. He spoke factually about the events that had supposedly occurred around them. Cliff asked who was watching them and writing down all the things they did, if they were the first two persons on earth. There was silence. Then the superintendent's face darkened. He called Cliff a trouble-maker and had him removed from the class.

Thus a life-long search for answers began. Cliff refused to accept a constraining view of life which others wanted to impose on him. Even today, he feels only a little closer to an answer to his innocent question, despite many discussions with a wide variety of knowledgeable persons.

Cliff's father was not a presence in his life, because he spent much of his time working or drinking with his friends. Many weekends, his father was the host for the town's floating craps game at their house. He would cover the dining room table with a large green felt cloth to use for throwing dice. The players bought whiskey and beer as the game progressed throughout the weekend. Cliff and Fern found ways to keep out of sight and keep themselves amused while the boisterous visitors took over the home.

One of Cliff's first encounters with a firearm was during one of many visits by the town's police officer, who enjoyed free drinks with his father. On one such occasion, the small child sat on the officer's knee playing with his pistol. Several men in the dining room were drinking and openly exchanging money over their game, unconcerned by the policeman's presence.

The excess of alcohol claimed his father's life when Cliff was seven. The Grade Two class bought flowers, and a sympathy card for the rest of his family. Cliff enjoyed several days off school, not yet comprehending the events. As he sat in the funeral parlor with his mother and sister for three days, his father lay quietly among the mass of flowers and cards.

"Why didn't he sit up? Why didn't he talk to his family? What had Cliff done wrong?"

By the end of the third day, Cliff understood.

During the funeral, Cliff was surprised and disgusted to see that many of those who had come to pay their respect had only gossip and harsh words for his father when he was alive. Worse, the minister, who had had no regard for his father during life, was now praising a man he had never met.

This struck the young boy as hypocrisy. He was angered. After the service, he waited with his mother and sister in the main hallway of the funeral home, as the pall-bearers closed the coffin and began to carry it outside for the ride to the cemetery.

As the procession passed the girl, she began to cry softly. In his unreasoning anger, the boy turned to her and said, "Don't you dare cry for him. Be brave."

Hazel was left destitute. With two children to care for, she found work in a local shoe factory. She arrived home each day worried and exhausted. The family had a house and garden to grow food, but little money. They got by on will and determination. The children sold strawberries, raspberries and potatoes from their garden. The money paid for school books and clothes that were needed from time to time.

The taunts of his schoolmates hurt, frustrated and angered Cliff. He gradually withdrew from them and became a loner. He took some solace in seeing himself as the man of the family. This role ended with his mother's remarriage and his legal step-father's moving into the house. Although it made life less difficult, Cliff had been deposed, so he built a wall between them. He became a loner also at home.

His teachers were not trained to deal with anyone who did not fit the mold. They showed no sensitivity to his stammer. Time after time, he would be sent to the front of the class to read aloud from one of the textbooks, only to stammer incoherently through a painful eternity. He would be admonished to shape up and ordered to his seat, amid the jeers of his classmates. He was sullen and withdrawn, yet relieved that the torment had ended. Each time this happened, he did not know how he could contain his outrage.

"Stammerers encounter problems in everyday communication that other persons never even have to consider. There is a sick feeling in the pit of the stomach. A cold, gripping ache, a hopeless fear of being asked a question in school. The stammerer knows that ridicule will follow any attempt to speak.

"There is even an inability to answer a telephone or a door-bell. A listener will invariably ask a stammerer to repeat what was said. That would cause me to freeze. No more words would come out.

"Some well-meaning persons attempt to help by out-guessing the speaker and telling him what he wants to say. Unfortunately, this also makes the problem worse. I would wonder why they could not wait a few seconds for me to finish what I was trying to say. Of course, I would withdraw further."

If he did not fit into society, then he would reject society, as it had rejected him. Laughed at for stammering, rejected by sports teams because he was small for his age and set apart at boy scout father-son dinners because he had no father, he did not want to belong to a social order that could isolate a person for being different.

He told himself that he was not lonely, he just preferred to be alone. He loved to hunt and fish. He felt close to nature. It seemed as if God were here somewhere. Even today, walking and communing with nature is a soothing balm for a worried or upset mind. Another reason Cliff played in the woods was to practice what he learned about woodland crafts and native Indian lore from the wonderful cards in cereal boxes. He spent hours becoming an expert tracker and woodsman. He could spend hours on his stomach cautiously stalking a ground hog.

By age 10 or 11, he would contentedly walk into the woods at dawn with a hunting bow and quiver of arrows not to be seen again by human eyes until well after dark. He would return tired and hungry but satisfied that he "had done his thing well" that day.

By sheer determination, Cliff managed to live with his stammer and the constant ridicule from his peers. He developed his own enjoyable interests. He learned to run for long hours and long distances. Alone in the fields or woods, he was happy. He was king.

Running became a major challenge for him. He ran everywhere he went throughout his teenage years. He found some acceptance in high school by winning mile races for his school and setting a record for the school district. He dreamed of outrunning Roger Bannister, the English runner, who set a world record by running a four-minute mile.

"When I was running, I was in control. On the track, no one told me what to do. I set my mind free as I ran. Often, after hitting the 'Runners' Wall', I could run for hours while my mind was at peace. This is a phenomenon that occurs after a time of strenuous running. In effect, the mind separates from the body and the body just continues to run without tiring."

***

The year Cliff completed Grade 10 was better than most years of his formal schooling, but school did not offer   nearly enough for him. If he was a student, he was a student of life, not of long-dead mathematicians and poets. After he became old enough to leave school and start a working life, nothing could hold him.

He started training at Spence Bakery learning baking and cake-decorating. The owners treated him well and taught him about the business. He enjoyed being paid for work that was eaten with enjoyment or admired as a wedding center-piece. Still, something was missing. He wanted a major change. On a shopping trip to Toronto, he was drawn to the navy recruiting center. The 18-year-old was accepted for training a month later.

As soon as the young recruits completed their travel to the naval base in Nova Scotia, culture shock began. The air was blue from the barked crudities of the commanders. There was a numbing sense that it was impossible to do the right thing. The desensitizing process was designed to separate the men from the boys, deemed "unfit for further service."   Only 65 from the original class of 160 took part in graduation six months later.

Cliff was assigned to the HMCS Buckingham, out of Digby, Nova Scotia, which took new entries in the navy out to sea for a week at a time. Then he was assigned to a ship out of Halifax, the provincial capital, which regularly traveled the eastern coast of North America from the Arctic Ocean to the Caribbean Sea. His second home ports were Bermuda and Boston. In the North Atlantic,   his ship followed Soviet submarines which were reportedly setting homing devices on the sea bottom, in order to navigate more easily to the coast. Occasionally, they would stop Soviet fishing trawlers at sea, board the vessels and inspect for weapons or electronic spying equipment.

During one tense encounter with a Soviet trawler, as armourer's mate on the Canadian navy destroyer, HMCS Algonquin, Cliff was ordered to hold the entire Russian crew at

14

the point of a Bren gun, while Canadian officers searched the vessel. The foreign sailors stood in a close group on the trawler's bow. Cliff covered them with the automatic weapon from the main deck of the Algonquin. To his relief, there was no trouble. Since nothing was found, the crew was released. Cliff was ordered to stand down his weapon.

The trawler moved away at normal speed, but after several miles, began to gather speed. Suddenly, a rooster-tail wake rose behind it as it disappeared rapidly over the horizon. Their radar clocked its speed at five or six times normal. There was more to that vessel than the boarding party had found.

One cold, punishing November night there was an exercise in the North Atlantic. Rain slashed the skin of the men on deck like ice. Ships maintained formation through fog patches with crew watching for "growlers", small icebergs that could easily punch holes in the sides of the ships. An aircraft carrier provided take-off and landing practice for planes. It sent a message to the rest of the convoy to watch for a plane that had ditched into the ocean during take-off.

Cliff's co-lookout shouted: "Object in water, bearing 30 degrees starboard."

Swinging his binoculars, Cliff spotted a man standing knee-deep in the ocean at a distance of almost five miles. Through the fog and rain, he spotted another man. Then another. Five in all. They were standing on the wing of their floating aircraft. The alarm was sounded. The message relayed to the admiral in charge of the exercise, on the carrier far ahead. Crews could only wait for the order to rescue the men. Seconds passed slowly and tension built. It seemed that the order to break formation for rescue would never come.

Finally the radio squawked into life.

Shock and disbelief at the unforgettable message.

"Maintain course."

Five men died in the exercise in the North Atlantic that horrible night. The incident is still with those who experienced it.

***

15

Is there window-dressing at sea?

One of the ships Cliff was assigned was required to escort the Royal Yacht Britannia from Halifax to Land's End, on the southwestern tip of England. Queen Elizabeth was returning to England from a tour of Canada. During the entire Atlantic crossing, the complete crew was required to wear white ceremonial uniforms at all times. Only someone who has plied the seas can understand the implications of wearing white at sea. The uniform picks up dirt from the continuous salt spray, from the ship's smokestack and seemingly from the very air.

Perhaps this was proper protocol, a mark of respect for the queen of the British Commonwealth. However, the crew was frustrated. Their comments were decidedly common. The queen's yacht was several miles astern of the ship. Unless she had very royal eyesight, indeed, she could not even see the men on the Canadian escort ship. Inspection of the dress of the day would have to wait for another time.

***

Cliff occasionally saw seamen who were injured or near death, usually from an accident or from a fight in a bar.

Often he would stare into the vast expanse of sky and water.

The questions again.

What happens when someone dies?

Why do some people suffer illness and others do not?

Why is it that some die young, for no seemingly good reason?

Why are we alive?

Would the naval chaplains have the answers?

Military chaplains were unlike other ministers because religious denominations meant almost nothing. They understood that men did what they did regardless of creed or doctrine. The men could approach the padres on an equal basis, freely and openly.

"We were respected equally by these fine men. Huddles on wind-swept darkened decks may not be the most likely places to get answers about life, love and death. But we had many long hours of earnest conversations. My encounters with a series of

16

these men, who had dedicated their lives to God, were always interesting and even fascinating. Yet somehow, I could not gain a real sense of satisfaction from their words and teachings.

"It seemed that I heard far too much supposition and far too many assumptions in the things they said. This approach was inadequate to explain the unknown. There was no certainty. I was attempting to find truth."

So Cliff's search continued.

***

In addition to the questions which seemed to be a part of Cliff, life on the Atlantic Ocean presented new kinds of mysteries. These would be marveled at alone or discussed with others and then put aside, waiting for answers.

* A huge waterspout appeared in the Caribbean Sea. A massive column of water, seemingly a mile high and a quarter mile wide, it moved rapidly across the turquoise sea and disappeared.
* A four-masted sailing vessel was sighted approximately two or three miles ahead on a foggy day in the Bermuda Triangle traveling at a right angle across the course of Cliff's ship. It disappeared in a patch of fog. Although it had not appeared on the ship's radar, a number of the crew reported the sighting. Was it the famed ghost ship The Flying Dutchman?
* Lightning struck Cliff's ship one especially stormy night a few miles north of Bermuda. He was stationed on the upper deck as a safety watchman in torrential rain. Suddenly there was a flash of light and a sizzling crack. All about Cliff, countless small blue flames appeared everywhere he could see on the ship. Flames around his feet. Flames all over the deck and superstructure of the ship. Yet strangely Cliff had no sense or feeling of electric shock from the blast of lightning.
* One warm, sunny day, Cliff's ship was part of firing exercises in a naval firing range north of Bermuda. All firing stopped when three American fighter aircraft approached from the East. The Canadian radio operators began to pick up transmissions between the aircraft and Kindley airbase in Bermuda. The planes had flown non-stop from California and were scheduled to land

at the American base. Each of the pilots was reporting low fuel supply and was concerned about having enough fuel to land safely. The pilots were told that they were cleared to land the best they could. The Canadian sailors watched from their position at sea as the first two aircraft made slow power-off banks and smoothly descended toward the distant runway, landing safely. The third plane began to bank slowly toward the base, then seemed to stop dead in the air. The plane turned nose-down and plunged straight into the sea, crashing in a huge spray of water. It dropped only a mile from the ship.

Emergency Stations!

Klaxon horns blaring, Cliff's ship steamed full throttle to the rescue. First at the scene within minutes, they found masses of bubbles rising from the sea bottom where the plane had gone down. One badly bent wing rocket and one empty flight boot floated on the surface.

Nothing else.

American helicopters arrived shortly from the base in Bermuda. They carried sonar searchers but found nothing of the pilot or the plane. The sea had completely swallowed a man and a plane and it just resumed its implacable, quiet rolling as if nothing had ever occurred.

***

In 1957, Cliff married Shirley, "a very nice Halifax girl" whom he had been dating steadily for almost two years. The wedding was held in an Anglican church on a lovely Friday evening in May. Within an hour of the ceremony, his bride underwent a complete character change. He would later learn that Shirley was struggling with an overpowering anger triggered by mental and emotional distress. In time, alcohol would aggravate the problem. Life became a series of arguments. Cliff became more withdrawn and depressed. His stammer worsened. He seemed unable to please his wife in any way. A son became his only relief. They spent many happy hours away from home, where the hostility and screaming could not reach them.

Near the end of his term in the navy, Cliff was asked to re-enlist for another five years. He signed the papers and returned home. An urgent message awaited him. His brother-in-law's wife had tuberculosis. Cliff and Shirley decided to go to Ontario to help care for the two small children. Fortunately, the navy had not yet forwarded his re-enlistment papers to Ottawa for processing.

Cliff hoped that their new life in Ontario with Shirley's family would help balance their life. However, things became worse. Cliff increasingly sought refuge outside the home.

He had always wanted to be a scuba diver. At 10, he and a friend had taken their maiden voyage into the world of deep-sea diving on the bottom of a creek. Their makeshift equipment included his stepfather's garden hose connected to a couple of large tin cans, used as a pump. Cliff tried it first. He put on a real diving mask. Slipping into the shallow water, he then put the end of the hose into his mouth. His friend began working the makeshift tin can pump. There was nothing at first. Then a strong taste of rubber and stale air. Success. All afternoon, they took turns pumping and diving, pumping and diving.

At home, they were told never to try that stupid stunt again. Their equipment was confiscated and the hose returned to garden duty. For the next few years, they limited their diving to mask and snorkel. However, their dream did not die. As adults, they trained and became skilled scuba divers.

Shortly after moving to Fort Erie, on the Canadian side of the Niagara River from Buffalo, Cliff heard the story of a father daily searching the river-bank for the body of his drowned son. The body was eventually recovered, but the father did not want anyone else to experience his weeks of uncertainty, watching and hoping. He successfully lobbied town council. The town started the volunteer Fort Erie Underwater Recovery Team as a unit within the fire department. Cliff joined and regularly searched for drowning victims.

Scuba diving replaced running and surpassed the woods as a spiritual retreat for the adult. Scuba diving became Cliff's life. It was a form of self expression, an outlet, and an opportunity to help others. He loved to dive and to teach others to dive.

"Diving became the closest thing to real spirituality and a way of being with God. Beneath the surface of the waters, there is a freedom of movement and a sense of oneness with one's own great spirit. The soaring above the rocks and the coasting on invisible currents that sweep one along, create a new perspective and a new way of learning.

"I believe it teaches personal spiritual satisfaction. Many times in my life when things seemed difficult or hopeless, I would submerge my body and soul beneath the healing waters. There I was free. I could move with the ease of thought. I was in control."

Even diving presented some new questions.

How did Cliff sense where to find drowning victims?

"One of the strange things about searching beneath the surface of the water for a body was that somehow I seemed intuitively to know where the body would be found. Inexplicably, I found myself drawn directly to the victim on numerous occasions. My instinct seemed to be well-honed, such as during those times as a child when I would crawl along the ground in the forest and ferret out unsuspecting creatures. I just 'knew' where they would be hiding."

Was he the only one who could see a glow around drowning victims?

"Often when searching for a victim, I noticed that a faint yellow glow appeared first. It seemed to emanate from the victim who came into sight second through the murky waters. Even while the body was still obscured from our view, the 'glow' could be used to direct the divers to the victim. This gave me more questions. What caused the glow? Do other divers notice a glow, or am I the only one?"

Years later, The Echo would say that the glow is the spirit essence of the victim that is visible to anyone who is sensitive.

The most troubling thing led to the end of Cliff's association with the diving recovery team in 1972.

"While answering an emergency call, I was driving my car to the building to gather my diving equipment. Somehow, some powerful force kept me driving past the building. Some thing or some strong impression influenced me so overwhelmingly that I returned to my home and did not dive at all that day. The sensation of impending doom was so intense that I stopped diving for the recovery team soon after."

From that time on, he took part only in occasional outings with a few trusted friends as diving partners.

He worked locally before obtaining immigration papers to start a job in Buffalo, with the Bernel Foam Company, a producer of polyurethane foam for the furniture and automotive industries.

Crossing the Peace Bridge on his way home one day after work, he was thinking that 1966 had brought some good things into his life. He liked his job and was to receive an increase in pay. He had even finished work early and would be home before supper. He stopped his car in the driveway and got out. He heard his wife raging and screaming epithets at their son. He rushed into the house to see his wife beating his son across the back with a hardwood chair rung. In one bound, he tore the stick from her hand and threw it out the window. He then swept his son into his arms. He would never let her touch their son again. She screamed at him to get out of her life.

Cliff moved into the Queen's Hotel, where he served drinks in the evenings as a second-job, after working days in Buffalo at this time. Within two years, his divorce was final. He was granted legal custody of his son.

The disastrous marriage brought back the questions.

Why do things happen the way they do?

What is the purpose of our lives?

He was determined to find an answer to some of his questions.

Chapter 2   Life as a psychic

The current rhythm of Cliff's life had begun after he and his second wife, Joyce, started living together in Fort Erie, in 1967. The young couple considered themselves "gloriously happy." Each had come from a difficult first marriage. They believed that they had finally found their lifetime mates. Cliff calls this period of his life "good and loving and comfortable. We began to build our future together."

The couple felt blessed with two wonderful sons. They had a house, a dog, and two cars.

"What more could one ask?"

Cliff had worked up to afternoon shift-supervisor from his initial job as a machine operator at Bernel Foam Company. His employment required him to travel between Fort Erie and Buffalo every workday for a number of years. He worked at the factory from 4 p.m. to 12 p.m. Joyce worked regular days in Fort Erie as a Canada Customs clerk. He and Joyce saw each other only in passing at breakfast or on weekends. For most of their 10 years together, Cliff cared for the boys during the day and Joyce cared for them during the evening.

Late in the marriage, Cliff began to notice some strange things.

Often, when he arrived home from work at 1 a.m. or 2 a.m., there was a dry spot on the road, surrounded by moisture, suggesting that a car parked regularly in front of the house for a period of time. Sometimes, the drapes and window blinds were pulled closed. Yet he and Joyce seldom drew the drapes across the windows.

One morning, Cliff called to talk to his wife at her workplace and was told that she had the day off. He was stunned. Joyce had left for work like any other workday, just an hour earlier.

Cliff's mind was uneasy. In the previous weeks, Joyce had spoken a great deal about a much-younger co-worker. Reluctantly, he considered this new piece of information. He had to find out. He drove to the co-worker's house. Joyce's car was parked beside the other man's car outside the house.

Cliff's knock on the door brought no response. Angrily, he launched a furious 15-minute assault on the door.

BAM BAM BAM BAM BAM BAM BAM BAM BAM BAM
BAM BAM BAM BAM BAM BAM BAM BAM BAM BAM

He continued until, finally, his ashen-faced wife came to the door. They agreed to go to a quiet place for a serious conversation. They talked for hours during that dreadful day. There were no apologies. Nothing was solved.

Cliff was devastated. His ideal marriage and his life had fallen apart.

Cliff and Joyce tried to continue living together civilly, no longer as a married couple. It failed. They agreed to part. He signed the house over to Joyce, instead of giving her monthly payments.

He gathered his few personal belongings, put his whole life into his car, and left. What was he going to do now? Where could he go? Was there a life for him somewhere?

He could not stay in Fort Erie. He had lost his wife, his sons from this marriage, and his familiar life. Even his dog was gone. His wife had sent that loving canine friend and protector of the boys to the pound. Fort Erie was a strange place for him now. Instead of comforting, it was mocking. He had to go somewhere new.

The answer was in Brampton, a city northwest of Toronto. There was a similar job waiting for him at Able Foam Co., if he would abandon 14 years of his working life in his job in Buffalo.

23

Brampton gave him Pat, a new female partner, who would help Cliff re-establish his life. However, job security and a stable life were illusory. After a few months, a brain tumor claimed the life of his new employer. The Able Foam production plant closed.

Somehow, Cliff managed to talk his way back into his former position with Bernel in Buffalo. The sad tale of his previous employer's demise bolstered his persuasive power.

With his old job back, all was as well as Cliff dare expect. Burying himself in his job was his way of dealing with his continuing problems. However, Cliff's life was becoming an Absurdist painting.

One January Friday in 1977, after Cliff had gone to work, it snowed in Buffalo. It snowed and snowed. The city slowed and then stopped. Cliff's factory lost all heat and power. Some of the employees had to be kept in the plant overnight. It was sure death for them to attempt to walk home.

Cliff was ordered to block the main exit doors with his body and let no one out of the building. All the employees were escorted to the upper floor of the main office, the building's second floor. Fortunately, the polyurethane foam produced in copious amounts at the plant could be pressed into service as emergency bedding. Slabs of foam were laid out in barracks-fashion for everyone to sleep on. Thin sheets of foam were used as blankets. About 30 employees weathered the storm that night in passable comfort while the "Blizzard of '77" blasted the building with winds estimated at the force of 40 kph (70 mph) and -70° F.

Around Saturday noon, some members of the Buffalo Fire Department, equipped with hand-drawn sleds, food and blankets, dug a passage to the factory door. They had come to help the employees to get to their homes in the paralyzed city. One at a time, the shivering, disoriented employees were loaded onto the sleds, swaddled in blankets and shuttled to their respective homes. A few hours later, the governor declared the city under Martial Law for the next week. Movement in the city was restricted to only those with authorized travel passes. Since Cliff was required at the factory, he was among several employees issued a pass. Several times, while driving to or from work, he was stopped by armed soldiers who carefully examined his pass before allowing him to continue on his way. Hovering overhead, military helicopters watched the proceedings.

The storm had passed. The city had begun digging itself out. Life was returning to almost normal. Except for the employees of Bernel. The factory building was heavily damaged. Frost destroyed the water systems and the electrical systems throughout the building. Production could not begin again until at least March. Most of the employees were laid off with little or no hope of ever returning. Cliff Preston, life's football, lost his job. He would not find employment again for almost two years.

It was time for the formal end of his second marriage. Cliff and Joyce decided to divorce with as little anger or argument as possible. They asked a local lawyer to handle both sides of their divorce. He was reluctant but agreed. The social cost of a divorce at that time was the admission of adultery by one spouse. In this case, the complication was the need to protect their sons from social stigma. If Cliff would bear the responsibility of being the villain, his sons and their mother may escape the full weight of society's disapproval. He agreed. Then Pat agreed to be named correspondent in Cliff's and Joyce's fiction.

Cliff drove to his estranged home. His estranged wife got into his car. They drove to court, appeared before a judge for 10 minutes, and then left the court building together as unmarried persons. They selected a quiet restaurant, and enjoyed a pleasant meal with agreeable conversation. They agreed to avoid speaking negatively about each other in the presence of their sons. They parted amicably, never to associate again.

For several years, he missed his sons terribly. Occasional visits intensified his pain. He was no longer a part of their lives. He asked himself what he had done to have his children isolated from him. He says that the sorry answer is…Nothing.

Soon, Joyce remarried. She talked Cliff into legally changing the last names of his sons to that of her new husband.

"For the boys' sake, Cliff," she said. "Think about how they will feel in school, if their name is not the same as mine."

Depressed, emotionally drained, and unable to think clearly, Cliff agreed. He signed the papers that changed the surname of his sons.

However, life was still not through playing cruel jokes on Cliff. Joyce's new husband died a mere six months after their marriage. Joyce had known him less than two years. Cliff's sons were left with the surname of a stranger, a man who had come in and out of their lives in a heartbeat of time. By contrast, Cliff is still haunted by the events during that period of his life which cost him his sons. Today he wishes only that he could turn back time.

"I would go back to the moment when I was asked to sign that flimsy piece of paper and I would tear it into a thousand pieces."

***

There were a few rays of sunshine in the darkness of 1977. Pat was one of the first. She had accompanied Cliff to Fort Erie from her home in Brampton. She shared every problem with him, helped him to believe in himself, and encouraged his psychic development. With no job and no family, Cliff finally turned to the psychic. He had nothing to lose.

He attended a weekend course advertised as a way to start becoming truly psychic. The course was presented by the Alpha State Mind Trainers, the young couple that Cliff had met at the psychic fair in Niagara Falls, New York, in 1975. To Cliff's delighted surprise, immediately after the amazing weekend, his life-long stammer had disappeared. He was starting to accept that he may have psychic powers. He was finally getting answers to his questions. He attended seminars, sometimes with new friends from the Alpha State weekend. He was learning to meditate, to quiet his mind and listen to his spirit.

One seminar was presented by Michael Blake Read, a deep-trance channeler from Toronto.

Blake Read lay on a reclining chair, beside a woman who directed him and monitored him. By accepting the softly spoken invitations to relax, to clear his mind, and to open himself to Spirit, he entered a sleep-like state.

The woman asked whether all was well with the entity.

26

A fascinating transformation took place.

A startling, unnatural voice came from the sleeping man's mouth. The strangeness of the voic e was almost frightening, but reassuring at the same time. The voice came from a place of absolute peace and absolute love.

The director called the voice "Evergreen."

She asked whether anyone had a question for Evergreen. A number of persons asked questions about themselves, or absent family members, or about business. Evergreen answered every question clearly and patiently. Cliff judged by the reactions of the questioners that the answers were accurate and useful.

Cliff was spell-bound.

He studied the sleeping form. He marveled at the stillness of the body and how it easily maintained this new persona. He was amazed at the clarity of the explanations in response to questions. It could not be the same man who had gone to sleep. Somehow, another intelligence must have replaced Blake Read. Cliff sat in awe of this loving and wonderful phenomenon.

The session lasted for approximately one hour.

Near the end of the session, the woman invited the sleeping man to "return to full awareness" and "be in the present, wide awake." Four or five minutes of gradual revival brought Blake Read back to full consciousness. He seemed to have little or no recall of any of the events of the last hour.

Cliff determined to talk to the man.

Talk they did. Eventually, he received all the necessary instructions to practice achieving trances of his own, including Blake Read's personal trance induction format.

The two years of unemployment were terribly difficult at the time. The experience teste d Cliff's limits. However, as he looks back on that period, he sees that the ordeal was necessary, and perhaps the only way that he could have developed as a deep-trance channeler. He had to devote a great deal of his time to succeed in this new pursuit. He needed to be free of outside constraints and distractions. He needed the determination of near-desperation. As always, he needed to find answers. It was increasingly evident that no one else had the answers to his questions. He was going to look for the answers within himself.

"It was a time of constant practice, of learning and growing internally. My lack of confidence as a child, which contributed greatly to my stammering, was gradually being replaced by a growing self-confidence. I was realizing my own worth. At last."

He was no longer afraid of what others thought. He learned to remove negative things such as judgmentalism from his thinking, He struggled to replace it with acceptance, understanding, and valuing of other persons for what they are, rather than rejecting and condemning them in his mind. He began to see the potential in himself and in others with whom he associated.

"I developed many new attributes of mind through my constant practice. I practiced at least once every day. Often I practiced twice a day and sometimes even three times a day. I worked constantly and doggedly with my director to develop the capacity for regular achievement of deep-trance states.

"Unlike some other channelers, who have experienced interventions of Spirit in their lives, I had no such sudden illumination or spontaneous appearance of trance entities taking over in my body. My formula was simple determination and hard work. There was nothing mystical or magical about my beginning as a deep-trance channeler."

In fact, Cliff's first attempts to learn channeling, were difficult and produced uneven results. He could not believe that any sounds which came from his voice box or any words which were formed by his mouth and lips could belong to any source other than himself. It took him a few years to develop the confidence that the altered voice and the knowledge produced in his channeling sessions come from beyond himself.

Cliff and Pat gave the source the name "Reflections of Echoes." In time the name was shortened to "The Echoes." Finally, Cliff settled on the name "The Echo". The source was agreeable to all of these names, saying that names are less important in the spiritual realm than individual, identifying energy vibrations. It has also said that spiritual entities have a name which is called a spirit name or eternal name, that is different from the name given to a person in the physical life.

28

For itself, the source has offered only the name "Golude", used to identify the spokesperson or spokespirit from the constantly changing group of resource spirits. Any one of these spirits may volunteer information in reply to questions. However, all the information is relayed through Golude, the group's one voice.

As this book was being written, The Echo recalled Cliff's attempt to learn channeling, in this manner:

"For a number of years, that named by Clifford, Echo, have waited in wings for the form to enter to that state of wakefulness at which it be available for we to speak.

This entity have, as it have viewed another entity in the performance of the channeling format, entered into decision that it will learn this format. At this point the entity be learning the art of deep meditation. This behoove the entity well for the deeper within self that one meditate the easier comparative it is for Spirit to speak.

The form of the one Clifford practice diligently with the assistance of another director and find that during the practice sessions it tend somewhat to lose perception of its location. At one moment in time the entity will hear its director speaking from far below it. The next moment from far above it and the next moment from beside it, where in fact the director is. This then gradually change to the point of which the entity do not in reality hear the director and may maintain some consciousness and wonder why it is speaking about a particular subject and what the original question was.

At another time the entity would hear a question and be unaware of the answer that was given. This then gradually progress to that point at which the entity decide that it be not performing as it in reality desire and at this point will not perform this format further.

This occur to the form Clifford during a practice session and the entity decide that this be its last session and that it no longer strive for this format. At that moment in time the mind of the entity be sufficiently open that we may fully enter and this be that which the entity state is a flash of light before its closed

29

eyes that it viewed as it were opening its eyes. Only after opening its eyes the entity realize that there be a time span of approximately one hour in duration of which it has no conscious memory. This be the opening to trance and the entity in following sessions find that it do maintain little or no memory and gradually to that point of no memory, allowing we of Spirit to speak freely and clearly through this open channel."

****

During Cliff's search that year for ways to find answers, he routinely talked to psychics. On one occasion he was talking to a professional psychic in Toronto when the conversation turned to tarot cards. The psychic asked Cliff to give him a tarot reading. Cliff knew almost nothing about this method of providing insights into individual lives. His hesitancy was overcome by the psychic's gentle encouragement.

"He told me just to relax and let my thoughts tell me what to say. I summoned all my courage and laid out the cards, that he had shuffled, in the pattern that came to mind. I just followed my instinct."

A tiny image on one of the cards drew Cliff's eye. It gave him an idea. He gave this idea to the other man. Another thought came to Cliff, then another and another. He was soon talking rapidly with little conscious thought about what he was saying. Yet, the information he relayed was accurate. He discovered that tarot can provide a means of communication between the conscious and the subconscious.

In a few weeks, Cliff found himself on the other side of a reader's table at a psychic fair. He, himself, was offering tarot card readings to members of the public. Later that year, the card readings would change to deep-trance channeling sessions, offered on an individual basis or a group basis.

He and Pat also began offering weekly "Open House" psychic information and meditation evenings, in Ridgeway, near Fort Erie. These sessions attracted guests from Toronto, Niagara region, Buffalo and even Erie, Pennsylvania. The small groups of guests held enthusiastic discussions often lasting until 1 a.m. and even 2 a.m.

Cliff went back to formal school for the first time since completing Grade 10 many years before. He trained as a stationary engineer at Niagara College. He went to work at the old YMCA/YWCA in nearby St. Catharines for two years as chief engineer and custodian. He left during the replacement of the entire staff when the secretary was found guilty of mishandling the Y's money. He next worked as stationary engineer at Niagara College main campus in Welland. After two years, he quit to pursue his first love - psychism, and work psychic fairs.

However, by early 1980 Cliff and Pat would agree to part because they were growing in separate directions. They remain on good terms.

Cliff's life on the road had started. He seemed to be filling a personal need by helping others to make sense of their lives.

Life on the psychic fair circuit was sometimes comparable to the life of a player in minor-league sports - too many wearying miles and absences from family and friends for fleeting, intangible returns. While fulfilling and rewarding in many ways, this way of life had none of the glamour or financial remuneration of today's well-known psychics. It could introduce hardship for many by exposing them to misunderstanding, hatred and abuse. At one fair in southwestern Ontario, two teenaged girls, wearing crosses and calling themselves "Born-again Christians", engaged Cliff in conversation. They talked to him for a few minutes before announcing that if he were reading tarot cards, he did not have the right to live because they claimed that the Bible advises do not suffer witches. He gave each 25 cents and said that after they had grown up they could give him a phone call.

Promotion was another part of a psychic reader's life. Usually, one or two readers would arrange interviews on local radio or television telephone-talk programs to publicize the event, offer free readings and entice the public to attend. This random method of promotion had varying results. Some shows were well attended, but many drew little interest and the participants barely met their costs or lost money.

One psychic fair which hit the participating psychics in their wallets especially stands out in memory. The fair, in southeastern Ontario, was sabotaged by a legal battle between the host hotel and the municipality. Local feeling was against the hotel chain in the dispute over waterfront property. There were only eight paying customers at the three-day event.

After paying for meals and lodging, four or five psychics, of the dozen or so at the fair, pooled their pocket change to purchase gasoline for one of the cars to transport the group back to familiar territory. The other cars were abandoned temporarily, to be retrieved individually when their owners were able to do so.

Somehow the psychics managed to rise above such disappointments. Perhaps it was being able to help people, the camaraderie or the satisfaction of doing work of their own choosing. Practicing psychism was not a job but a way of life.

**

After Cliff and Linda Bevington attended a friend's wedding in August, 1980, as friends, they became serious about each other. Linda had been a guest at many of Cliff's weekly open house sessions in Ridgeway in 1978. She had next agreed to accompany her current mother-in-law to an evening of psychic readings at a nearby mind awareness centre, although she did not believe in psychic things. Several weeks later, Linda watched in fascination as Cliff performed one of his first public channeling sessions. She even saw a spirit near the feet of Cliff's comatose form. In 1979, a private channeling session changed her life. By now her marriage had ended. This was one of the things she asked about. The Echo's comments helped her understand what had happened in her marriage and helped her adopt a positive attitude about her life.

In February, 1981, Cliff and Linda were married in Welland, by a justice of the peace with two close friends as witnesses. They had postponed their original plan of a marriage in May because of a growing guest list of friends. With more time to plan a wedding and a reception with a larger number of guests, during good weather, they remarried in May, near the beautiful town of Niagara-on-the-Lake. The reception was at their apartment in Niagara Falls, Ontario.

During this period, Linda was learning to acknowledge that the highly unusual events in her life were signs of her advanced degree of psychic ability. She could also acknowledge that the signs came from Spirit. Once as a child of about five, she had gone to sleep in her bed and had awakened crying in the front hall of the apartment building, outside locked doors. She was told it had been a dream. Years later her mother gave her the facts. She had gone to sleep in one place and somehow her sleeping form had materialized in another part of the building. She had not awakened and walked to the other location. No one had carried her there. Years later The Echo would tell her that she had transported her body.

Once as a young adult, she was in one part of a building and suddenly she was in another part. She had no recollection how she had arrived there. A minister called it a miracle. The Echo would tell her that this was another occasion on which she had transported her body.

As Linda began developing an understanding of psychic things and grew comfortable with her new outlook on life, she had accepted a role that would have seemed inconceivable not long before. She became the director for a local channeler. She assisted him as he went into trance and made sure that he was at ease and in no danger from any source. She assisted clients with questions and answers. She determined when the trance session should end and then assisted the channeler back to full consciousness.

With these credentials, Linda naturally took a full role in a combined psychic life with Cliff. She became Cliff's director for his deep-trance sessions. Cliff and The Echo also encouraged Linda to develop her own psychic powers, nudging her first in the direction of numerology. She was entering a frugal life with Cliff, which sometimes brought economic hardship. However, they were committed to spiritualism and felt wealthy and certain of themselves as long as they were together and could extend generosity to others who were in more difficult circumstances. When the four or five psychics carpooled home following the unsuccessful psychic fair in southeastern Ontario, it was Cliff and Linda who drove the others and shared their home overnight with one of the passengers.

Soon after their marriage, Cliff and Linda began playing host to a group of friends who arrived for weekly meetings to meditate and discuss things related to psychism and metaphysics. Somehow their landlord acquired one of their business cards and assumed that they were running a business from their apartment. They received an eviction notice. At the time, they took part in psychic fairs almost every weekend. Their telephone was for personal use and to contact promoters only. However, they refused to argue with their landlord, and moved to a townhouse in Chippawa.

Cliff left his job as a stationary engineer at Niagara College main campus in Welland because the psychic work was becoming much better. However, within a few months, it shrank dramatically because of their relocation and their lack of a telephone for approximately one month. They were unable to pay their rent and had to leave between Christmas, 1982 and New Year's Day, 1983.

A couple they had met during a fair offered them space in their home near Picton, Ontario. It was a wonderful offer, but how to get there without sufficient money? Another friend lent them a small school bus, that had been converted to a camper, for the Prestons to move their belongings. With the bus loaded and Linda following in their car, Cliff drove on Highway 401, sometimes at less than 50 kph (30 mph) on hills. They arrived safely at the farmhouse, where they spent a frugal winter, as the host couple was also struggling financially. The two couples successfully met spring by sharing resources.

The farmhouse served as their base for the spring and summer of 1983, as they worked fairs in such various locations as Toronto, Hamilton or London. In the fall, Linda organized their own fair at Quinte Mall, in Belleville. This success led to their decision to begin traveling with their own fair. With a van and a horse trailer for their tables and curtain set-ups, they traveled northerly through Ontario to such locations as North Bay, Sudbury, Sault St. Marie, and Thunder Bay. They drove through Manitoba without doing any shows because a residency law prevented them. They spent several weeks in Regina, Saskatchewan. Despite a positive reception, the sour note was the theft of Linda's purse in the mall's women's restroom. It was never found. She lost several hundred dollars and her identification records. When the Prestons went to a federal government office to acquire new documentation for Linda, they were delayed by unrealistic government requirements. It was some time before they managed to settle the matter in an acceptable manner. Next stop was Calgary, Alberta. The city wanted a $2,000 bond. It would be $500 each for Cliff, Linda, and the two other psychics traveling with them, to work in the municipality. So the Prestons drove south to Lethbridge where the local mall manager welcomed them. For a reasonable rental fee, they opened on Monday morning. Business was good. Linda made a successful television appearance on Tuesday morning. However, by Tuesday afternoon, protesters calling themselves "Born-again Christians" were picketing the mall and threatening drivers entering the parking lot with perdition if they even talked to the Prestons. The young, inexperienced manager asked the Prestons to leave, despite a petition by the store owners for them to stay because they were good for business. They accepted a refund and closed their fair.

The next day, they were invited to breakfast with a well-known Canadian sociologist, and his class, at a local university. They were encouraged to take a stand against the protesters. However, the Prestons saw no benefit in this suggestion, as they wanted to assist those with open minds, rather than squabble with those with closed minds. They continued to Vancouver, British Columbia, where they stayed for a time with Linda's parents.

Chapter 3   Life in the Canadian Arctic

In 1988, Cliff was a stationary engineer at the Dufferin Area Hospital in Orangeville, Ontario. Was there a subconscious desire for a break from serving others through psychic work? Did he want to change something in his life? One day as he read the newspaper, he noticed an advertisement for a stationary engineer position in the Northwest Territories (now called Nunuvut). He was not sure of the reasons that he replied to the ad because he did not think that he would even be considered.

There was a surprise telephone call a month later. It was a preliminary interview for the position. A week later, in a second telephone interview, Cliff spoke to more territorial government officials. During a third telephone call, he was informed that an airline ticket to Rankin Inlet, Northwest Territories, was available for him at the Toronto airport. Cliff and Linda decided that the opportunity was worth more investigation. At least Cliff would be able to see Canada's far North, if nothing came of a personal interview. The population of Rankin Inlet was approximately 1,500 at the time, including 300 southerners.

Cliff flew to Winnipeg, Manitoba on the first part of his journey. While waiting for his transfer flight to Rankin Inlet, he met another candidate for the position. The other stationary engineer was from Vancouver. He was also looking for some indefinable change or missing element in his life. A man and woman in Inuit clothing were the only other passengers on the 1,500 km (900-mile) flight. The flight attendant and the four passengers had a friendly two-hour conversation. It was a pleasant introduction to the Arctic.

Below, the endless forest finally gave way to a flat, snow-covered vista. Rankin Inlet appeared as a cluster of buildings, huddled together in the vast whiteness. As the rear door of the plane opened, a blast of cold air hit Cliff.

"What was he getting himself in for?"

He pulled his coat tight and walked down the stairs from the plane. He gasped as the sharp cold air filled his lungs. He rushed across the tarmac and into the warm welcome of the small airport waiting-room.

Confusion. A number of persons in parkas were milling about and receiving baggage and parcels. They were speaking a strange language that Cliff later learned is Inuktutut, the native language of the Inuit.

A Northwest Territories government official met Cliff and the other candidate and took them to the hotel. As they became settled in their rooms, Cliff took a photograph of the washroom to prove to Linda that the toilets were indoor. Then a tour of the town, less than 1.6 km (1 mile) wide. The roads were gravel and without sidewalks. Most of the houses were single-family saltbox-style that had been issued by the federal government. There were three schools, one for small children, the second for teenagers, and the third was residential. They were also shown the Hudson Bay Company store and the co-op store, which contained a range of articles from food to clothing to supplies for dogsleds. The mine head of an abandoned nickel mine could be seen standing like a sentinel near the shores of the inlet.

The residents considered the temperature of -20° C (-4° F) warm for November.

After the job interviews at the territorial government offices that evening, the other candidate told Cliff, "If you want to work here, you can. But I do not." Cliff, however, was interested. He thought that he and Linda could live with the Inuit in a northern Canadian town.

The return flight to Winnipeg stopped in several Inuit villages on the way south. The first landing was in Whale Cove, approximately 80 km (50 miles) south of Rankin Inlet. An Inuit family's five-year-old son sat next to Cliff. As the plane circled to land in Churchill, Manitoba. The little boy was now occupying the window seat. He asked Cliff about the green things in the snow.

Cliff realized that the small and sparse trees far below the plane were enough to fascinate a boy from the tundra. He had never seen trees before. Many of the things most Canadians take for granted are not available to the people of the far North. Although Cliff had traveled from the east coast to the west coast of Canada, the North seemed like a different world for him, as it would for many other Canadians. Cliff was proud to be part of the boy's learning experience.

The plane reached Winnipeg several minutes late. Since the airport had delayed the departure of the connecting Toronto flight, the breathless passengers rushed from one plane to the next. Before all the passengers were secure in their seats, the plane began to taxi to the main runway for takeoff.

Cliff was back in Toronto seven hours after leaving Canada's high Arctic. Would not the explorers of the past be amazed? Such distance required them to deal with extreme hardship and months of travel. Modern travelers cover the distance in less time than a normal workday.

Cliff and Linda lived in the Arctic from January, 1989 until January, 1992. They welcomed the adventure and used it as an opportunity to recharge their spiritual batteries. They had not left a forwarding address when they moved from southern Ontario. Furthermore, in Rankin Inlet, they did not speak of their past as psychics. They did not advertise or seek psychic work. However, psychic work sought them. Somehow, some people found them and they received telephone requests for long-distance deep-trance consultations with The Echo from London, England; from Georgia, USA; from Greece; and from Finland.

Perhaps they appeared secretive to one suspicious acquaintance, who was also a temporary resident of the north. She wanted to know whether they were in a witness-protection program. In time, she became a close friend.

The three main adjustments for the Prestons were the isolation, the harsh weather and living with the Inuit, a new culture for them. The isolation was eased by cable television which offered many stations from a satellite relay. Residents could receive such faraway television stations as Vancouver, Winnipeg, and Hamilton, Ontario, in addition to some American stations. On radio, they could listen to a range of programs, including such exotic things as broadcasts from Russia, which had anecdotal value rather than practical value. However, cable television was expensive, as were most consumer goods and services. Most things were flown in from Winnipeg, approximately 1,500 km (900 miles) away. They had to pay more than $1,000 for a television set. All fresh food was flown in, at a premium price. Choice of affordable vegetables was lacking and the cold weather made special demands on human bodies, so Linda temporarily gave up vegetarianism and began eating fish and chicken again.

The weather in Rankin Inlet is almost year-round winter. Spring seems to last for about a week in early July. Then suddenly it is summer. The temperature moderates but seldom gets hot. After the snow melts, children may be seen swimming in melt pools during the short summer. Mosquitoes appear in vast numbers and travel over the now-soft boggy land is almost impossible. By the end of September, winter begins to reassert itself. Almost-constant wind picks up the snow, creating a wind-blown cloud of snow that rises to a level of about 12 m (40 feet) above the ground.

It took time for The Prestons to get used to these strong, frequent winds. The first week, they saw two young Inuit children go outside to play during one windy period. The children held onto some pipes rising from the ground. As their tiny bodies were lifted almost at right angles to the pipes and pulled in the other direction, their laughing faces were not visible to the newcomers. The Prestons told them it was too dangerous to be outside, and brought them inside. Later, they learned that this was a normal way for children to play in this harsh land.

The Prestons each had a frightening experience with the weather that could have been fatal.

For Linda, a routine trip to the post office turned dangerous. Although she would not call the strong winds blowing snow that day a storm, she was not used to the winds. She pulled the hood of her parka over her face and walked with the winds at her back. On the way home, she assumed she would have to walk into the winds. After walking for some time she suddenly tripped and fell over a huddled dog, part of a sled team kept by its owner on the ice covering the bay. She pushed back her hood and saw that she had been walking out over the frozen bay and away from the community.

Tripping over the team was a Godsend. The wind was so strong that she would have continued walking away from safety, had she not fallen. Although she was able to walk back to town, she felt lost and unsettled. No one had noticed her because no one else considered the blowing snow especially bad. Her usual 10-minute trip took an hour.

For Cliff, the frightening experience started as a routine trip by snowmobile to feed his sled dogs in their compound, about 50 m (50 yards) away. After he set out, the snow and wind grew worse. Visibility dropped to only 2 m (six feet). He became disoriented in the driving snow, losing his sense of direction and even becoming unable to tell when he was moving. When he realized that he was in danger, he decided that his dogs could wait another day to be fed. Turning the snowmobile around, he was uncertain where his apartment building would be found, as he drove slowly ahead.

Why could he not find his building? How could he miss it? After several minutes, he saw the dull orange glow of a light, which he hoped marked his building. He put his arm out and felt something solid. This must be his building. He kept his hand on the solid surface as he slowly manoeuvred his vehicle around the corner and the side of the building to the safety of the entrance.

The quality of light in the Arctic seemed intense to them. In winter, the extreme thickness of the clouds created a novel condition in which there were no shadows. Without shadows, people have very little depth perception, so they could bump into snow banks before seeing them. There was never complete darkness at night because of the snow. The full moon seemed much bigger than they were used to.

The Aurora Borealis, popularly called the Northern Lights, made a sensational display for approximately 30 minutes some nights, beginning with a fizzing or sizzling sound in the air. The community's dogs took little notice of the lights. However, there was something which caused the dogs to react. A change in atmospheric pressure led to an eerie event. It seemed that every dog - hundreds of dogs in all - howled for four-to-five minutes, starting and stopping simultaneously.

The Inuit name for themselves in Inuktutut means The People. They are a proud, self-sufficient people, spread around the top of the globe in many different countries. They are also courageous, resourceful and practical.

Cliff says that the strongest influence in Arctic communities was the family in power. One or two influential families exerted unchallenged social power in many northern Inuit communities. In Rankin Inlet, the hamlet council, run mostly by the elders, prevailed upon the cable television service not to relay programs from one American station, because they considered the programs too violent. The operators of the service agreed to this censorship because the alternative was to be shunned by the leading family, the worst possible insult.

Spirituality is a mixture of Christian religions and traditional shamanism. Despite their strength of character, many residents were fearful of shamans and were reluctant to talk about the subject. Cliff suggests that some residents believe that if someone has powers to do good, he or she may also use the powers for harm.

Linda says that shortly after she arrived in Rankin Inlet, she had a vision of a shaman in her living room. She could sense whenever a shaman had come to the village and she says that the visitor always knew that she knew. She herself was called shaman by a young Christian Inuit woman who sought Linda's "healing hands" to get relief from intense pain. The woman suffered from muscle pain, toothache, and abdominal pain. She appreciated Linda's hands-on help but was fearful of her. A Cree native man, who was living in Rankin Inlet, also asked for Linda's help whenever he was injured.

The Prestons became loving owners of sled dogs. Most native residents owned dogs as a matter of course and sometimes neglected to feed them. Some owners killed their young dogs at about 10 weeks of age, for the fur coats. Since frost does not adhere to dog fur, it makes perfect trim for parkas. Cliff and Linda stood out in their treatment of dogs, gradually accumulating 24 healthy dogs. They imported food from Winnipeg and mixed powdered egg with the regular food to improve their dogs' coats. People sometimes gave them dogs but it also worked the other way. Cliff was aware that covetous eyes sometimes fell on their dogs. One day, two of his pups disappeared from their compound. The next morning during coffee break in the government lunch room, Cliff stood striking a 2x4 piece of wood in his hand and announced that someone had stolen two of his dogs. He said he was going to knock on every door in town that night until he found his dogs. He said he would have given them away, but that no one was going to steal his dogs from him. His Inuit co-workers showed no expression and said nothing. Cliff had no intention of using the wood, but he knew that a direct method was necessary to get attention. It paid off. By feeding time at 5 p.m., the two pups were back with their mother.

Linda learned to drive a snowmobile and Cliff learned to drive a dog team. She also learned that she can communicate telepathically with dogs. They taught their dogs to pull a sled with Linda leading the way on the snowmobile and sending a mental picture of what she wanted of the dogs. Cliff drove the sled. On a day that they were using a one-two-two-two formation, one of the dogs in the second two was not pulling its weight. The lead dog stopped the team. It turned back, jumped over the first pair of dogs and trounced the slacker. Cliff thought it was a fight and he wanted to stop it. Linda said the lead dog was just using a form of discipline. Soon order returned as the chastened dog co-operated. However, the slacker used the same technique of letting the lines slacken to escape the harness, on another occasion. When Cliff went after the wayward dog, the rest of his team ran away and needed rounding up. Although he achieved some degree of skill driving sled dogs, Cliff said he would always be cautious when driving a team because the dogs would always attempt to do what they wanted, and had to be watched closely at all times.

Linda's influence with dogs was also useful when she taught a mother dog how to take an occasional break from her nursing puppies. Linda visualized on only one occasion, the dog jumping on top of the dog house and then jumping on top of the wire fence and walking over the top of the next section of the pen and then jumping down to the ground. She visualized the dog returning by the opposite route. The dog quickly learned what Linda pictured.

The same mother dog had its hind legs frozen in the snow in January after giving birth and instinctively curling around the puppies in the snow. Cliff used his axe and ice pick to remove the dog. When he saw the serious damage, he put his rifle against the dog's head and was ready to end its suffering. However, he hesitated. He thought that it deserved to live because it had been a good dog. He lowered his rifle and set the dog free. It hobbled around on three legs until mid-summer and then it seemed to be back to normal. The Inuit who had thought that he did not know what he was doing and had urged him to shoot the dog, probably took no notice now. Experience told them that he should have shot the dog and saved himself trouble with it.

Life in the Arctic taught the Prestons things about themselves that they might not have learned otherwise. It taught them to look at life differently and to realize the validity of how other people live.

One of Linda's lasting impressions of life in Rankin Inlet is the strength and self-reliance of the people who can live in the North and do not need Whites. The harsh climate made her see that people had to kill animals, for food and clothing.

Cliff is impressed that the Inuit can live by themselves or in groups. "They are intelligent and ingenious. They can make things out of almost nothing. They have a Spartan life but if they are handed lemons, they make lemonade."

An Inuit whom Cliff worked with in Whale Cove shot a polar bear in his back yard. Cliff asked him about it some time later. He answered in the Inuit matter-of-fact manner that he had to shoot the bear. He caught it eating his dog.

On another occasion, a member of one of the influential families was in a hunting expedition at the edge of the ice over Hudson Bay, 50 km (30 miles) away from shore. All but one of several persons who were in their tiny six-foot wooden punts, rushed to the safety of solid ice after they speared a walrus and it submerged. The greatest danger is not knowing where the angry 450 kg (1,000-pound) walrus will surface.

One Inuit man stayed with his boat. He was standing when the walrus surfaced underneath him, lifting his boat out of the water. The punt rested precariously on the wounded monster's back. The other hunters fired some shots and killed the walrus.

Asked about the incident, the following day, the man confessed, in the typical Inuit manner: "I was nearly scared."

Hunting takes great skill, courage and determination. Hunting polar bears by snowmobile is an example. The Inuit in one community had 11 licences to shoot polar bears. They worked steadily during one night tracking the polar bears on the soft, flexible saltwater ice in Hudson's Bay, 1.6 km (1 mile) off shore. The bears walk carefully with their legs spread as the sheets of ice rise and fall. The drivers judge the precise speed needed to keep their vehicles' runners on the ice. Too fast means the runners could thrust under the sheets of ice and drop the vehicles down into the water. Too slow means that the weight of the snowmobile could crack through the half-inch ice and plunge the driver into the water. When a hunter is close to a bear he steadies his rifle and shoots the bear. Then he circles back, lassos the bear and tows it to shore. The take that night was the full quota. Bears are used for meat and hides. Most pelts were sold to the Canadian government and sent south. Some hides were kept. The front legs and attached chest could be used as warm, water-repellant leggings. Often with no other clothing worn underneath.

As the commander of the Civil Air Search and Rescue organization, for the eastern Arctic, Cliff also did search and rescue work. On one occasion a teenaged Inuit boy went missing. Searchers using air spotters and snowmobiles located his dog team but had to give up searching for the teenager. A week after he was reported missing, he walked into the Royal Canadian Mounted Police station showing no ill effects of his ordeal.

Cliff was not sure whether he was impressed by the youth's courage, self-reliance, or, was it luck?

***

Cliff and Linda were loosely planning to remain in the Arctic for another 15 years, but they heard about a farm for sale outside Winnipeg. The down payment was in their price range. They started daydreaming about the things it could give them – a peaceful life close to nature, answering to no one but themselves, moving to their own inner voices. The ideal appealed to them. They would have to be decisive about buying the farm and act quickly. They had lived in Rankin Inlet for almost three years. It was a special experience that they would always remember, but perhaps it was time to move on.

However, their decision was complicated because they were slightly short of the three-year-employment requirement for the federal government to pay two thirds of their considerable moving expenses. A full four years - just slightly more than one more year - would be necessary to receive full payment of their moving expenses. They asked The Echo for advice. The Echo said that they were free to move but advised against buying the farm. They were also assured that they would be able to meet the employment requirement of three years, but if they stayed for more than one extra week, Cliff "would miss his life's path."

With this intriguing prophesy in mind, which seemed like a spiritual cue to action, they moved 1,500 km (900 miles) south to Winnipeg. Cliff spotted an advertisement in a newspaper and felt a compelling attraction to a weekend program in Time Line Therapy™ (TLT), a process which takes a client's subconscious mind back to the point of origin of a present-day problem, and then brings it forward free of the problem. Cliff saw this as another possible way of helping people.

"All my life I have been interested in people. That was a real opportunity to help people, which did not involve several years of university to learn a narrow focus," he explained later.

He was the top student in the program and enjoyed the experience so much that he took eight months of training from the same instructor in another new field, Neurolinguistic Programming (NLP), which included hypnotherapy. NLP uses the client's own personal creative and visual references to ensure that the mind receives only positive information. An image of the person as whole and perfect is presented. Negative words are avoided. The purpose is to alter thought processes and assist the client's mind in solving the client's problem.

Next the Prestons moved across the Ontario border to Fort Frances. Cliff taught stationary engineering at the local community college, while planning to return to their familiar Niagara region in southern Ontario. Here he would re-establish his psychic practice and begin a counseling service, as a separate venture, offering all three therapies. In time, he would decide that he was most effective with TLT™.

"It doesn't matter what the client consciously believes. The client's mind finds a solution and the therapy works. With all three approaches, the client's mind is always in control. If the client has been experiencing problems, the reason is that the mind allows these things."

Eventually the Prestons sold their possessions, and came south in their car with their computer and two dogs. Fortune briefly smiled on them. First they were able to stay with friends until they found their own place. Next another friend offered a house at a nominal rent, because she was also a friend of Hugh-Lynn Cayce, a son of Edgar Cayce, who had been one of Cliff's models and inspirations. Cliff asked the Ontario government about the legality of practicing hypnotherapy, a therapeutic procedure long misunderstood which was only recently becoming respectable. After a long wait for a response, he learned that it had been legal during his wait. He could begin offering hypnotherapy services, with TLT™ and NLP, as another practical method for clients to overcome their negative thinking and unwanted habits.

However, the Prestons would have to put much of their lives on hold later that year, as Linda contracted encephalitis and her neurologist believed the illness would be fatal.

Chapter 4   Linda overcomes encephalitis

This chapter is from Cliff Preston's personal diary, written at the time that his wife, Linda, contracted encephalitis and miraculously recovered after her doctors had given up hope. These are his original courageous and moving words. Minor editing is for clarity and consistency.

We discussed the purpose of including such deeply personal material in this book. Cliff and Linda believe that it is important to show the healing power of love.

September, 1994

Lately, my wife, Linda seems to be going through some kind of emotional upset, withdrawing from me, pulling into herself. When I approached her to talk, she wouldn't listen, she wouldn't talk about the things going on inside of her.

"And besides," she reproached me, "You never listen to me, anyway!"

This was not like Linda. Normally, she was bright and cheery and happy, easy to talk with and simply loved engaging in long discussions with me. Something was wrong. I was at my wit's end, and didn't know how to help her, let alone approach her. I loved her so much, yet somehow she seemed to think that I was in opposition to all her thoughts and ideas!

This was the general atmosphere during the early days of September, 1994. Little did I realize that her withdrawal was the harbinger of much more serious difficulties to come!

If I had only been more vigilant, then perhaps things could have turned out differently.

As a couple, Linda and I were inseparable. We had been married at that time, for 12 years, both coming from other failed relationships. We spent most of our time together, working in our chosen fields and complementing each other in our work.

Recently, Linda had begun doing Kripalu Bodywork Massage sessions out of a local hair salon, and thoroughly enjoyed it. Through time, through her persistence, and because she loved what she was doing, she was able to build up her clientele to a satisfying degree.

It was mid-September. Linda began to develop symptoms of what appeared to be a common flu. She began to sleep a great deal and became listless and lethargic when she was awake.

Simple tasks such as making a meal or cleaning the house became such difficult chores, she would abandon them and retire to the bedroom.

Linda continued in this state until the early morning hours of September 24, 1994. Since she had been sleeping so fitfully, I had made a point of checking on her each hour, both day and night. After checking again at 2 A.M, and finding that she appeared to be resting comfortably, I became involved in some work on the computer and did not return to the bedroom again.

A short time later, Linda came to the door of the computer room and stood staring at me for a moment. I asked her how she was doing and her reply was a clear, "I'm fine".

With this, she turned and went back to the bedroom.

Somehow, I felt that things were not quite right. So, following her to the bedroom, I looked down upon her, lying on the bed, and asked again if she was alright.

Linda replied, **"What are those two men doing in the corner?"**

"What men?" I asked, a sudden shock running through my body!

Something was horribly wrong!

Leaning over, to look closer, it soon became evident to me that her eyes were staring and vacant.

Another cold chill ran through my body!

Seemingly, Linda was intently studying a spot high above her head and off to the right. And then she began to repeat over and over again, as if in a chant,

"Oh   my   God,   Oh   my   God,   Oh   my God"!...

By this time, I was in a near panic, and so I grabbed her and shook her, calling Linda!.....Linda!.... but it was useless.

She just kept repeating, "Oh my God" over and over again.

I tried calling her name again. No Response!

Again and again, I called her, as if my will and my voice could still the incessant chanting and restore her to the cheery, bright, healthy Linda I knew and adored.

Still no response!

Linda grew silent, and lay staring at that same non-existent point above her head.

The telephone! Call for help, I thought to myself. I rushed to the living room for the phone!

The 911 operator answered with a maddening calmness.

"Police or Ambulance, sir", "Thank you, sir", "Hold the line Please".

I was calling for help! My mind screamed out at her, "my wife needs help! Where do you think I'm going"?

I sat with Linda while interminable minute after minute passed by.

The ambulance.....will they never arrive?

Then...Flashing lights ......men coming into the house.......loading Linda on a gurney.......asking which hospital to take her to....the closest, of course!

Even in the face of my angry panic, those capable men of the ambulance service did their jobs well.

Linda, the woman I love, arrived at the hospital in minutes!

THE STORM HAD BEGUN !

Day, September 24, 1994

The ambulance had taken her to Hotel Dieu emergency room and they immediately called a neurologist to see her.
By 4 a.m., they took her to the General Hospital for a CAT scan and brought her back to Hotel Dieu. At this time a spinal tap was performed and the neurologist told me to prepare for the worst.

51

She said the spinal fluid sample was rampant with viral infection and this meant that Linda...my wonderful partner Linda... had ENCEPHALITIS!! The doctor held out very little hope, and told me to start calling the family, as she might not live past noon!

I really thought Linda would be soon in spirit!

They had to paralyze her breathing in order to help to stabilize her, so Linda was put on a breathing pump in the Intensive Care Unit on the fifth floor. She was also given lots of antibiotics to attempt to stay the infection.

Retiring to the hospital quiet room, I attempted to think of my next step, without success. I was tired and confused, but even more strongly, I was angry.

How dare they tell me my loving wife is dying?

What has she ever done to deserve this?

Angry. Angry. Angry.

I closed the door of the quiet room, so I could be alone. Then, remembering the strong belief that Linda had in Sri Sathya Sai Baba, I asked aloud if there really is a power such as Sai Baba, now would be a good time to show it to me.

[Author's note: Earlier the same year, Linda had become interested in Sai Baba, considered by many to be an avatar and a living saint. He is credited with such miracles as healing, bilocation, and materialization.]

A figure slowly manifested before me. In that tiny waiting room, I saw a small man dressed in a red robe, take form. He appeared for only a few seconds, smiling a loving smile at me, then slowly faded from view.

Suddenly, magically, I knew what must be done. I reached for the telephone and began calling all of the alternative practitioners I could think of to come to Linda's aid.

Close friends came to the hospital early on that Saturday morning, and gave me some support, and then we returned to our house where I went to bed while my friends made phone calls for me to people I felt should Know. I went to bed around 11 a.m. and woke up in time to get back to the hospital before 3 p.m. When I arrived at the hospital, another loving friend was already sitting with Linda in the ICU.

Others were waiting outside the intensive care unit and these persons I escorted to Linda's side. One of the nurses stepped before us and said, "You are only allowed one visitor at a time." Lifting the nurse aside, I told her " You have given up on my wife, but we will not, these people are practitioners, not visitors." All the rest of that day, Linda was never alone. Someone continually had a hand on her, touching her, as I thought that if she felt completely alone, she would just withdraw and cross to spirit. Others were applying massage, polarity therapy to establish a protective energy field around Linda, cleansing her aura, and just plain human love throughout the day and into the following morning. Whether someone else would believe in these treatments does not matter to me, because they worked.

By 4 p.m. Linda's eyes opened for the first time that day. By evening, she was awake, but very disoriented and with obvious memory losses. She could not speak due to the breathing tube in her throat, but she could communicate with a gentle hand squeeze or slight movement of her head. I stayed with her until 1 a.m. Sunday and then went to a friend's place to spend the night.

Sunday morning. I went home to feed the dog and to get cleaned up a bit and then went back to the hospital until around 4 p.m. By this time I was getting really tired so went home to sleep.

7.15 a.m. I just called the hospital to find out how Linda is doing, and her nurse said she tried to jump out of bed during the night to go to the bathroom. In doing so, she fell and hit her head. The doctor ordered x-rays and she is all right, although she has a goose egg on her head.

Linda....Linda, my love, are you trying to leave? Please stay with me.

I love you so and I miss you more than you can ever know. I love you.

I love you...I love you. I love you. I love you...I love you.. I love you.

When I arrived at the hospital, Linda was very bright and talkative. She is having some difficulty with her memory, both short and long term, but I think that will improve in the next few days. Linda has improved so very, very much! I am so pleased at her speedy recovery and at the people that have rallied around her...there have been hundreds of them! GOD BLESS THEM ALL!

TUESDAY, SEPT. 27, 1994
Today ***** was at the hospital in the afternoon for a couple of hours.

I went there around 11 a.m., left for lunch and went back again around two, leaving for supper at about 4.30 p.m. Friends were in around supper time to do a Reiki treatment for Linda, and then I went back at about 7 p.m. and stayed until 8.

Linda is in process of figuring out what happened to her, and she knows that she has some memory losses, so I think that is a good sign.

A comment I heard this morning about Linda....."I haven't known Linda for very long, but there are some people you meet that you instinctively just know are SPECIAL PEOPLE. Linda is one of those. She is full of love and always willing to help someone out. She really is one of the most special people I've ever met". (N. R.)

THURSDAY, SEPT. 29, 1994

Went to the hospital in the morning for about an hour, then came home and had some lunch, then went back to the hospital to see Linda.

I gave her a back rub and she went off to sleep, so I left again.

I'm beginning to get very tired now...I guess the word is exhausted!

Linda will likely be going to the regular wards sometime tomorrow, as they are just waiting for a bed in the right location......near the nurse's station, where they can watch her. Her memory is still very spotty and she is getting frustrated with losing the conversation sometimes.

FRIDAY, SEPT. 30, 1994

Last day of September, so I think we can now get on with new beginnings and Linda and I can start a new era of our life together.

I called the hospital at 8.30 AM, and the nurse told me Linda pulled her I.V. out during the night, but is ok and is slated for transfer to the ward as soon as a bed is available. Thank God and all the wonderful people that were praying and performing healing circles for her!!

We only know wonderful, loving people, it seems!

END OF SEPTEMBER 1994

OCTOBER '94

SATURDAY, OCTOBER 1, 1994

This morning I took in some family photos to see if I can twig some more memories for her and help her get her memory back in quicker time.

Our landlady called and wants me to go with her to hear some Christian Healers speak in Niagara Falls this afternoon. I think I will go with her, and see what this is all about. She says they sometimes speak in tongues..

I listened to all the speakers at the Foxhead Hotel in the Falls...they are not saying anything very different than we do, only crediting it to an outside source.

I did get an absentee healing done on Linda by one faith healer who was doing a number of healings there today.

WEDNESDAY, OCT.5, 1994

I spoke to the Doctor this AM and she said Linda is doing well, in fact she said "its a miracle she is alive at all". She is arranging for physiotherapy and a speech therapist to work with Linda. Also, she is sending her to Hamilton for a day to have an MRI done (Magnetic Resonance Indicator). This will let us know if there is any permanent damage in the brain..... I don't think there is, as Linda's memory is improving daily.

I told Linda this afternoon, that I had found a good home for our male dog, Toby..... she thought I had waited until she was sick to get rid of the dogs! This couldn't be further from the truth, I love those dogs! Not knowing how long Linda is going to be sick, I can't be concerned about the dogs. Linda is my only real concern.....

I MUST find and use every way possible to help her out of this difficulty!

OCTOBER 6, TUESDAY, 1994

This morning, when I went to the hospital to see Linda, the hospital staff were doing a mock evacuation and there was a lot of confusion everywhere.

Linda has more colour in her face today, and is concerned about her dry skin, so I showed her where her moisturizer lotion is kept, and she used some on her face! Good sign to me that she is coming along really well, now. Also, she ate a very good lunch. She ate all of the fruit with dinner, plus a pear that had been brought by a friend.

I have just had lunch at home and am headed back to the hospital in a few minutes. I can feel myself beginning to become

exhausted, so am now beginning the slow-down process since this thing may go on for a long time,
I don't need to be sick while I'm taking care of my love Linda.

FRIDAY, OCT.7 ,1994
I stopped at the hospital this morning on my way to do an HYPNOSIS/TLT™ session. Linda looked a little tired and was somewhat frightened when the physiotherapists came to take her for a walk. She (I think) had visions of more needles or other painful treatments. I reassured her and then left to do the session.

When I returned to the hospital, I found that a couple of friends had been there and had taken Linda in a wheel-chair and gone outside for a few moments in the bright sunshine. Linda was really tired after this and seemed to be even more disjointed in her thoughts. I think we will have to be very careful of any stress we place upon her for some time!!

Right now, she is fully aware of what she wants to say, but either she suddenly forgets it, or she cannot put the words in proper order. As an example, she was reading a newspaper, and I asked her about the story she was reading. She threw the paper down in angry frustration and said "It doesn't matter, I am not compensating anyway".

She meant to say "not comprehending". Often a word she uses will be the union of two other words and will not make logical sense to the listener except if the listener is very attentive to her line of thought.

Saturday, October 8, 1994
It's been two weeks today that Linda went into hospital. Her recovery to this date is phenomenal...Sat. Sept. 24, the doctor told me she was dying, most likely before noon. Well, she didn't and I think it was because she always had someone who loved her, touching her throughout the entire crisis! She was so surrounded with the powerful love of all her friends and close

loving family and of course me, that there were no openings for spirit to claim her.

I LOVE LINDA SO MUCH!! I WILL SEE HER THROUGH THIS AND BACK TO GOOD HEALTH AS SOON AS POSSIBLE! I SWEAR IT!

SHOCK!!!!!

I went into the hospital around 10.45 am. and the nurses were taking Linda for a shower. The nurse told me that Linda had had no breakfast and did not respond to anyone in any way. After her shower, Linda sat in the wheel chair staring at me and then into space, as though not seeing anything at all. I held her hand and talked to her for an hour and a half with little or no response, then got the nurses to help me get her back in bed. Once in bed, she seemed to be more relaxed, but the vacant stare remained, along with the non-responsiveness.

A doctor was called in by the nurses, because Linda began to have hand and face convulsions (7 in one hour, that I kept track of).The doctor said these convulsions are often a permanent part of the individual after such a serious bout with Encephalitis, so she ordered an IV in Linda's arm and began feeding her this way, as well as a mixture of dilatin and phenobarbatol to control the convulsions.
I left the hospital around 3 p.m., as my emotions were running far too high for me to be useful. Loving friends were with her, and promised to stay with her until she stabilized, anyway.

WHERE TO GO FROM HERE?

Sunday, Oct.9, 1994
I got a message in the a.m., from the hospital and called back. It seems that Linda, under the effects of the drugs she is on, has been trying to climb out of bed and they needed my ok to put restraints on her. Not reaching me, they moved her bed to a location where they could see her from the nursing station.

9 p.m.... I've been at the hospital all day with Linda. She is in a private room now, much more quiet and comfortable for her. Since yesterday there have been some changes...she now has more difficulty in forming her words. She wants to know how long this illness is going to last, and her question is " OK,shlow shlow losh shlow?". She knows what it is she wants to say, but cannot form the words, and this is very frustrating for her.

I have been giving her only positive input and have been very careful NOT to say things like "You remember", or "remember when".

She is often apologizing for being sick and causing trouble, but I assure her there is no trouble when it comes to taking care of her because .....

...............................I LOVE HER..........!!!!!!!!!!!!.

I finally broke down at the hospital this morning, and it was such a little thing that finally did it. I was combing Linda's hair and noticed how much more white there is in it in the last couple of weeks. For some reason, this just made my heart go out to her, as she seemed so frail and vulnerable. I broke down in tears and went and hung out the window for a few minutes until I could bring myself under control once more.

My main concern was that Linda did not see me crying, as it might affect her in a negative manner. I try to keep a happy face around her in order to maintain her sense of confidence in a return to health.

MONDAY, OCTOBER 10, 1994...........THANKSGIVING DAY.......
Crystal clear sky and sunshine greeted me when I woke. Thanksgiving Day !
This is the day that Linda and I would have been returning from Thunder Bay, Ontario.

I guess some things just don't work out the way they are planned.

59

THANKSGIVING.....I have a lot to be thankful for right now.

.... Linda has pulled through a tremendous trauma and is well on the way to healing now.

.... We are so rich in TRUE FRIENDS, that often my mind is boggled by the things people are doing for Linda and I in our time of need.

.... I still have my health and am able to help my love Linda when she is in such need of loving care.

.... I still have clients calling for appointments, so I can still make a comfortable living for us.

I went to the hospital in the a.m. and made sure Linda had a good dinner. She ate everything on her tray, and we talked for a while, even though her words are garbled, I still found I could decipher what she was trying to convey.

There is nothing wrong with her thought processes, it's just bringing the co-ordination to her tongue and right hand.

I feel confident we can beat this little difficulty.

6.00 PM. .********** came over at lunch-time to be here when I had my client in at 1.00. The client, arrived on time and I did a regression session with her. She left around 2.30 and ********* and I went over the "Keys" course material together, as she is going to help me with it this week-end,

I now have four people registered for the "Keys" for this Friday.

OPEN HOUSE.....12 persons were here for the open house and we did a healing cycle, one-card readings and then an energy circle that was pure power! Most of this energy was aimed at Linda, so she should be feeling pretty good now.

TUESDAY, OCT.11, 1994

When I went to the hospital this morning, Linda was sitting in the chair next to her bed and had been for quite a while. She remained there until after her lunch and then I called a nurse to help me get her to bed. She was asleep before her head hit the pillow.

I returned around 3.30 and she was still sleeping. The Doctor came in to see her, but we could not wake her. The doctor said to make sure she got her medicine when she did wake up, and then left.

A friend showed up and fed her supper and Linda was very talkative...she seems to be able to form her words a little better today, as I and our friend could understand her quite well.

Tonight, I have a client for Hypnosis.

SUNDAY, OCT.16, 1994

I haven't written in this diary since last Tuesday.

Since that, I have done three hypnosis sessions, an "Echo" party and a "Keys" course. I have also been going to the hospital steadily every day.

Today, Linda seems to be a little clearer in her speech, and she even sat up in bed and made some jokes.

Along with her stubbornness, her sense of humor will see her through this.

WEDNESDAY, OCT. 19, 1994

3 p.m., I have just finished with a client, and now I'm trying to get a phone call through to the doctor. Linda was taken to the General Hospital this morning for a Cat-scan, and I want to know what the prognosis is from that. I'll be at the hospital in a little while anyway, but I seldom get to see the doctor.

Linda's mother called last night to see how she is and sends all her love to Linda.

Linda was especially chipper this afternoon, asking me about the old farmhouse at Bolton where we lived in 1984. I was pleasantly surprised to hear her memory working in that manner. It may be that she will entirely recover from this insidious sickness.

THURSDAY, OCT. 20, 1994

I had a client this morning for a Tarot reading and then I went to the hospital and sat with Linda all afternoon, until 5.30 p.m. She was not quite so active as yesterday, but still she is improving, speaking more logically now each day. I love her so!

Together, we will beat this!

OCT. 22, 1994 SATURDAY
I just finished a Tarot reading for a lady who hunted me down from months ago.
Now it's off to the hospital to see my love, hope she is doing well today. She was so much better yesterday, that I'm greatly encouraged that she will achieve full recovery from this illness.

COME ON, LOVE, FIGHT! WE'RE ALL FIGHTING WITH YOU!

I LOVE YOU.....I LOVE YOU......I LOVE YOU....

Went out to Port Robinson this afternoon after I left Linda at the hospital and attended a friend's Fall Fair at her church.
When I went back to the hospital, close friends were there, and Linda was talking very well and very intelligibly. I came home around 6:30.
At about 9 , I received a phone call, and when I answered........IT WAS LINDA CALLING ME !

She said my voice sounded strange on the telephone and was I sure I was Cliff? I assured her I am, and she said she needed her glasses if she was to read the new Sai Baba book I took to her.
I went right to the hospital, and found Linda was sleeping soundly, so I left her glasses on the table next to her bed.
If she remembers calling me when I go in tomorrow, it will be a major breakthrough in this illness! COME ON LINDA MY LOVE! MY LOVE!

Sunday, Oct. 23, 1994
When I got to the hospital, Linda was crying and reached out for me like I was her saviour! She was all upset because she wanted out of the hospital ... right now!

I took her for a ride around the building in the wheel chair and that tired her some and she went back to bed.

Later, a friend came in and read to her for a while, then after some sleep, I read to her and then left around 8 p.m.

At 10.P.M., I got another phone call from her, just to wish me goodnight.!
She's coming along!!!

Monday, Oct. 24,1994
Today, I gave Linda a full body massage with massage oil, and this seemed to really help the aggravation feelings in her legs. She slept for a while when I was reading a book on Sai Baba , and then we went for a wheel-chair ride around the hospital for about 20 minutes. The ride tired her, but she said it was a good tiredness, and was asking how her sons, Rick and David, were doing out west, and if they had found work yet. This would indicate to me that at least some of her memory is returning,....slowly....but it is returning. She also asked if we had any dogs left now, to which I said "no", and Linda said "I guess you found good homes for them". I left it at that.

The Doctor called around four o'clock and said the CAT scan showed some brain damage on the left side, but very little pressure in the head and that she was very pleased at the way Linda is responding and how fast she is responding. The Doctor is attempting to get the medication balanced to the proper proportions for Linda's make-up as soon as possible. This should then allow Linda to balance and live a normal life.

OCT. 25, 1994.
This morning I went to the hospital around 9 a.m. and Linda and I talked for a long time. She was telling me all the spiritual reasons why this illness has struck her. Her memory was very good today, and I took her for a ride around the hospital in the wheel chair, gave her a massage and read some Sai Baba to her.

The physiotherapists came and took her for a walk down the hall-way just as I was leaving to get ready for an Echo party.

OCT. 26 LINDA'S FIFTY-FIRST BIRTHDAY !

I got her two new night dresses to wear in the hospital and a new house-coat, When I went in the morning, I took her a huge cluster of helium balloons in all bright colors to brighten up her day.

A friend gave her a cup with the flower for October on it and Linda was thrilled! I stayed with her all day and up to the end of visiting hours in the evening. The hospital kitchen staff sent up a small carrot-cake with whipped cream on it and some party decorations.....and a single candle in the middle of the cake!

I lit the candle and Linda made a wish and blew it out (with a little help). It was a very good day!

OCT. 27, 1994

Today Linda is very bright and active, she is still weak, but her mind seems to be working very clearly. We talked most of the day and she is now getting concerned about how I'm keeping the house, and how I'm managing with all the bills. This shows me that her mental processes are working quite well and she just needs to have some loving help to get her speech all straightened out.

During the evening, I took her for a half-hour ride around the hospital in the wheel-chair and she was interested in almost everything, stopping to look at a medical chart of the foot and noticing how a metal ankle is put together. I left for home around 8 p.m..

OCT. 28, 1994 FRIDAY

I spent nearly all day with Linda and we had some wonderful conversations about a variety of things. She had a number of visitors, today. All came in to say hello, and she was very receptive to them.

After supper, around 7.30 P.M., a couple of nurses came in and said they were changing her room because they had a couple of men coming in and needed the room.

Within 10 minutes, they had moved all her things and her bed into another room.

The sudden shock, change of scene and lack of a bulletin board for her cards seemed to really threaten her security.

Suddenly, Linda was remembering all the belongings we lost when we moved from Fort Frances to southern Ontario, and was wanting to know where they are now. "Why is that bowl not here?", was one of the many questions she shot at me.

Poor Linda... She does not understand what is happening and this leaves her frightened and causes her to regress to where she was last week! I just wish the hospital staff would let her stay in one spot! Since she arrived at Hotel Dieu, she has been in four different rooms. I.C.U., 323, 322, and now 324. Each time she is moved, she thinks she is being sent to the "dying room".

END OF OCTOBER 1994

NOVEMBER '94

First day of November, 1994, and it is raining. There was a terrible thunderstorm during the night accompanied by torrential rains. Now it's 9 a.m. and still raining outside.

Linda has (yesterday) reached a decision that she must work very hard if she is to find a way out of this problem, so she has begun to attempt to read everything she sees and to pronounce each word correctly. I repeat the words to her until she can say them right and then move on to another. She is doing remarkably well in her reading and is also walking much better now, also practicing this several times daily by walking out into the hallway and back to her room with me supporting her by the arm. She is getting stronger each day and her language is a little bit clearer each day.

There is a speech therapist that shows up once a week, but I'm not sure at all that a once a week encounter is anywhere near enough to even get to know Linda!

I'm going to find some books that have large print and get Linda reading these in order to help her return to her old wonderful curious self. I am looking for ways to stimulate her mind to cause her to become even more curious and determined to beat this thing.

At the hospital today, Linda was in very good shape! She had her shower this morning and went for a walk with the physiotherapists.

This afternoon, she and I walked the entire length of the hall on two separate occasions! Linda's strength is rapidly growing, and now she wants only to get out of that place! This evening, she was pleading with me to let her come home, and all I could do was tell her I would speak to the doctor.

Nearly broke my heart!

I had her looking at photos too, and writing down the names of the people she knew in each photo. This seems to be working rather well, as I notice that when we went over the photos a few hours later, she remembered most of the names easily.

In our conversations today, Linda often mentioned names and places from the past, and when I first went in to the hospital, she was writing in the diary I left there.

Her written words were " Today I remembered the names of my sons...Richard and David."

THURSDAY NOVEMBER 3, 1994

Linda had a little setback this afternoon. Suddenly, she became chilled to the bone and could not get warm no matter how many blankets I piled on her! I had the nurse check to see if her medication had been changed or missed, and they took her blood pressure and temperature, finding this to be normal!

I massaged her arms legs and back for about an hour and the chill finally left, just as rapidly as it struck. A few minutes later, Linda was sitting up talking with the speech therapist.

The speech therapist, was very pleased with the way Linda has advanced in the last week, and told Linda this before she left.

A short time later, the Doctor came in and sat talking to Linda for a while, noticing the dramatic changes also.

Later, the Doctor told me she is applying for a spot for Linda at Shaver Hospital, next to Niagara Rehab. Centre, to get her in there so she can have proper re-training and care.

MY CONCERN IS: HOW LONG WILL SHE HAVE TO BE THERE BEFORE I CAN TAKE HER HOME?

I feel that if she fights staying in the rehab centre, it may break her spirit, and she will retreat into herself. Then she will not allow herself to recover, and just stay there indefinitely. !

NOV. 5, 1994 SATURDAY
Today Linda walked the hallway in the hospital about 10 times and is she ever stepping out! The nurses are pleased with her and one nurse told her this morning that most people don't get over this illness so fast. That it usually takes a year or two for people to heal!

NOV. 6, 1994
I called Linda at the hospital around 9.00 A.M. and she sounded to be really bright and happy. She said she had just had her shower and she walked all the way to the shower and back again by herself! MAJOR SUCCESS!
I had an Echo party today, so I didn't get to the hospital until almost suppertime. Linda and I talked and went walking in the hallways and when she became tired, I left to come home.

NOV. 7, 1994
Today I signed the papers to apply for a spot for Linda at the Niagara rehabilitation centre, Shaver Hospital.

NOV.8 ,1994
Yesterday, the hospital staff put an old very sick lady into the bed next to Linda, and the lady was groaning and whining loudly.
During the night, Linda, not being able to sleep, got up from bed and with a pillow and blanket, began a trek down the hallway (unaided) to find some other place to sleep! One of the nurses

found her and returned her to her bed and moved the old lady into the hall so Linda could sleep.

The result of not sleeping was that Linda had a very bad day today, she only walked with the physiotherapist for about five minutes and had to be returned, tired and shaking, to her bed.

I took her in for her bath this afternoon, and that short walk tired her out desperately and she slept soundly after that.

I stayed with her until 9 p.m.

NOV. 9, 1994

Spent all day with Linda at the hospital. The social worker, came in and told us that if I talked to the head nurse, I could probably get Linda a day-pass. The head nurse said she was going to speak to the Doctor because of Linda's rapid recovery, and we could have a pass that would allow us to take Linda out any time she was feeling well enough.

This could lead to Linda staying at home and only going into rehab during the day.

Linda asked me today if I still loved her when she is like this......

Until that moment, I don't think I realized how much I really do love her!

There was a sudden feeling like my heart went out to this lovely lady that I am sharing life with and the feeling included all the wonderful things we have done together over the years. Also there was the sense of love for her in her present state and her extreme vulnerability.

I love her more now than ever!!!! This lovely lady is the other part of my life, as I hope I am of hers.

DO I LOVE YOU? YOU BET I DO !

LINDA MY LOVE !

NOV. 11, 1994

68

THIS IS DAY 49 OF LINDA'S HOSPITAL STAY !

Yesterday, the doctor signed the order to allow Linda to have day passes to come home for a while on days that she is feeling good. This could lead to her coming home soon and we would then have home workers come in to give her physiotherapy and speech therapy.

If that works out ok, she may not even need to go to the Niagara Rehab Centre at all.

Today, I'm going to bring her home for a couple of hours to let her re-orient herself to the house. I'm looking forward to having my love back in her own home again !

Over the last few days, Linda's memory has been returning at a phenomenal rate. She has remembered things about people from our Monday night group and even their past history!

Each day it seems to be returning more and more and she is retaining more of what she has remembered also.

Well, Linda really enjoyed her trip home! I noticed that she had a lot of memory about the city as we drove through it and almost total memory about everything in the house. She navigated the steps easily and made her way around home with no difficulty. The most important thing for her was to have a bath in her own tub! She also directed an Echo session in the living room.

I signed her out of the hospital at 12.30 and brought her back at 4 p.m., and this seemed to be enough for her for this time.

I am teaching the Keys course all this weekend, so I won't see her again now until Sunday evening, but a friend is going to spend most of the weekend with her.

Thank God for friends! They have been priceless throughout this entire wild episode!

THURSDAY, NOV. 17, 1994 ....DAY 55 LINDA'S HOSPITAL STAY

9 a.m. ...Just received a call from Linda that she can leave the hospital today! I am going in now to find out about her medicines and home care and all that kind of stuff!

OOOOH HAPPPPPY DAAAY! OH HAPPY DAY!

69

MY LOVE IS HOME AGAIN!

LINDA.... I LOVE YOU WITH ALL MY HEART AND SOUL !!!!!!!!!!!!!!

NOV. 19, 1994 FRIDAY

Linda came home from the hospital on Friday, Nov. 18, 1994.

All we had to be concerned about was her medicines, which I picked up at Shopper's Drug Mart on Ontario and Lakeport.

She is so happy to be home, and I'm soooooo happy she is home!!

I'm teaching the Deep Trance Workshop this week-end, so Linda has opted to stay in her room, as she doesn't want to see a lot of people just yet.

A friend is coming over on Saturday and Sunday to take Linda for a drive and some sight-seeing for the afternoon. This will break the monotony for her as I can't be with her right now and teach the course too.

This friend has been a tremendous help throughout this entire episode!!!!!

I wonder sometimes how I could have coped if she had not been around as much as she has.

Thank You *******, in case I forget to tell you!

The Deep Trance Course is going very well, at least Friday went well. We'll see how Sat. and Sun. go.

MON. NOV. 21, 1994

Well, the Deep Trance Workshop went very well! All of the participants said they were extremely pleased with all aspects of the program!

Today Linda and I have some running around to do in town. Linda seems to feel better when she can get out and change the view and see different things. The new sights seem to stimulate her memory and she begins to bring up old memories that I thought were lost forever!

She is improving every day, and it is like she is learning everything from the beginning all over again.

Tonight, during the open house, I went to the bedroom to check on Linda. She did not take part in the evening as the rush of people was too much for her to handle. Linda slept like a baby all night.

WED. NOV. 23. 1994

This morning we woke to the first snowfall of the year...lasted 'till around 10 a.m.

Linda's Occupational Therapist made her first visit at 9 this morning, and Linda really liked her and is looking forward to her next visit.

We went for a walk through the back streets to the lake in the morning and then I had a client in the early afternoon for Hypnosis.

SUNDAY, NOV. 27, 1994

This last week has been really a learning experience for us both. Linda has been hanging on to her very strong belief in Sai Baba, and this is certainly helping her on her road to recovery. She talks openly to Sai Baba at any time, and seems to be getting helpful information that is aiding her in coping with the problems of understanding and her mobility.

The speech therapist comes on Tuesday, the occupational therapist on Wednesday, and now the physiotherapist will be coming on Mondays. It seems to me that these people are really quite helpful, even if they only show up once a week. During the rest of the week, I can supply whatever therapies Linda can deal with, as I'm here all the time with her.

Sunday Nov. 27, 1994

This morning, it is now 10 a.m. and Linda is still sleeping. I expect she will waken soon and we will have breakfast and then do some walking later.

The day has come with beautiful sunlight and clear skies, although it is on the cool side with the temperature around freezing.

I woke Linda at about 11 a.m. and she was extremely slow in moving and getting out of bed. Also she was very agitated, as she swore that had I not awakened her right then, she would have died! The dream she was in at the time was one of moving on to spirit in the next minute or so, just as I woke her. This is why she was so stiff and sore and slow in getting out of bed!

Monday, Nov. 28, 1994
We got up at 7 a.m. today as Linda now swears that she must never get more than eight hours of sleep, or she will never wake up. She is adamant that she rise at 7 a.m.. and retire at 11 p.m....
We have to go out and do some shopping today as the larder is beginning to look a little bare, and we have the Monday night meditation group at 7 p.m.
The physiotherapist is due to call at 3 p.m. also.

Some time later
I was reading some of Linda's questions to The Echo that were written just shortly after her return from hospital in Nov.1994
"How long before I am long old naterlie? My smiling is so bad that later I don't know what I asked. Please help me. I dry so hart."
"lgnesh...when will I speak better?"
"Wickness..of no strecth..I am so weak"
"right now, I right something spell wrong. When I go back I don't know what it makes. How long before I will Know everything?

These are some of the kinds of questions Linda was writing as her mind was fighting to return to a "normal" state. I read these this morning and they brought me to tears, realizing how close my love has come to never returning!!

72

Chapter 5   Signs from Spirit?

This chapter presents several inexplicable incidents from different periods during Cliff Preston's life. Are these incidents signs from Spirit?

* A ghost in old San Juan

When Cliff was in the Canadian navy, shore leave in San Juan, Puerto Rico turned into a bar fight. Terrified at seeing knives and hearing shouts of "Kill him", Cliff ran out into the street. Five angry men chased the former high school runner, as he ran the most important race of his life through the dark and deserted streets of the old city. But he could not lose them. In desperation, he turned into a covered alley about as long as a city-block. Catching his breath half-way in, he glanced back and glimpsed his pursuers.

He turned forward to continue running as a tiny, brilliant light appeared in the darkness ahead. Cliff froze. The light grew larger and brighter. It took the shape of a man's head and the features of a face ? his father's face. It hovered slightly above eye level and smiled at Cliff. In a clear, distinct voice the face said, "Don't worry." It shrank to a tiny sparkle of light and disappeared. The episode took only a second or two, time that Cliff did not have. Tensing for action, he looked back again at his pursuers. They were not there. Cliff was alone in the dark and silent alley. His fear had gone too. He cautiously made his way back to his ship without incident.

As this book was being written, The Echo replied to a question about what gave Cliff the determination to learn channeling.

73

The reply included the following comment on the incident in San Juan:

"This also be a degree of push from we. As we be prior stated waiting in the wings. We offer to this entity a beginning point in that of the year 1958-59 by allowing the entity to view the face of its male parent while the entity be in danger and the danger vanishing. This be done in order to assist the entity in opening. However, the entity be of stubborn format and require a degree of time in the life of the entity."

* Gold chain and crystal pendant.

One morning, Cliff awoke to find the chain and crystal pendant that he seldom removed from his neck lying in place on his bed, as if it were still around his neck. The clasp on the chain was still fastened. How could the chain fall off his neck during the night, re-clasp itself and spread itself out?

* Mother's tri-light lamp

Cliff repaired a tri-light floor lamp that had been in his mother's home for most of his childhood and teen-age years. He placed it behind his living room sofa, since it was mostly decorative. It stood there unused for several years. One night as he walked into the living room, the lamp turned on for a few minutes and then blinked off. Cliff spent several more minutes attempting to turn it on again. No luck. Annoyed, he leaned over the sofa to pull the cord out of the electrical socket in the wall so the lamp would not act up again. He looked down at the cord and socket in amazement. The cord had been unplugged the whole time that the lamp turned on by itself.

* The disappearing book

One morning Cliff was reading a borrowed book on psychic phenomena. When it was time to prepare lunch, he put the book in a small basket that sat atop the chest freezer in the kitchen. It would be safe there until he could return to it shortly. However, needing to look in the freezer, he put the basket and book aside, removed items from the freezer and placed them on top. After finding what he wanted, he replaced the items in the freezer and the basket and book back on top. He ate lunch alone, with the rest of his family at work or in school. After eating, he reached for the book. It was gone. He searched the house but still could not find the book on psychic phenomena. Later that day the whole family searched in vain. Two weeks later, as Cliff was looking for a reference book in the floor-to-ceiling bookcase in the living room, he put his hand on a book on the top shelf. The missing book. It was turned pages out, rather than spine out. No one knew how it had gotten there, title hidden.

* Footsteps

Arriving home early one morning, Cliff and his wife were almost asleep when stealthy footsteps could be heard overhead, as if someone were walking across the attic. They started upright in bed. Was there a burglar? The footsteps seemed to be nearing the attic door, so Cliff crept to the door at the bottom of the attic stairs. Feeling anger, Cliff planned to grab the unseen intruder. Adrenaline pumping and heart pounding, Cliff would pull the door open at the first touch of the doorknob. The steps were coming closer and closer. The last step. This was it. Cliff was ready. Suddenly the sound of the footsteps was beside him. He could hear the sound move around him and retreat down the stairs to the first floor. He and his wife heard the footsteps clearly but no one was there. They were calm now and felt only amazement. There was no fear. This sequence of events repeated many times during the next few years. They learned to accept it as one of the characteristics of the house and ignore it.

* The vanishing lady

Cliff began getting drowsy while reading in the upstairs den. He put his book down and fell asleep on the sofa. His wife was working downstairs in the kitchen. Cliff awoke after a brief sleep, sat up and put his feet on the floor. He looked around the room. To his surprise, there was an old woman in the rocking chair opposite him. She appeared old and wrinkled, in a dark gray Quaker-style dress with a white apron. A lace-trimmed dust cap on her head covered gray hair. Motionless, she stared out the window, ignoring Cliff. His mind raced. Had they met? What is her name? It must be one of his wife's relatives. Cliff stood and politely introduced himself. The startled visitor snapped her head around in the direction of the greeting. She peered at Cliff with wide, fathomless, black eyes. Then she vanished. Cliff was extending his hand in greeting to empty air. Shocked, he jumped back, almost falling over the sofa. He ran downstairs to tell his wife that her relative had vanished. His wife had no knowledge of any visiting relative.

A few days later, Cliff asked their minister about the incident. Someone trained in spiritual matters would be helpful. Mistake. The minister said that Cliff was suffering from mental stress and delusions. He offered to find Cliff a psychiatrist. Cliff simply walked away as the other man was talking. Cliff found his answers elsewhere and never associated with any church again. For several years the Prestons could occasionally feel a cold spot in the room. Cliff could even keep his hand in the cold spot as it moved slowly about the room.

* Ghost in the nursery

After the birth of their first child, the Prestons redecorated the front, upstairs bedroom where Cliff had seen the vanishing lady. The crib was near the door for visibility from their bedroom. Cliff and his wife took turns checking the baby during the night when it cried. One early morning, after a particularly trying and tiring day, Cliff did not have the energy to move when the baby cried. Cliff asked his equally tired wife whether she could check their son. She agreed. However, this time they both fell asleep again.

Several hours later, they awoke in unison. With a guilty start, they ran to the nursery. Their son was sleeping peacefully next to an empty milk bottle. The bottle had been left full on the corner table on the far side of the room. How had the bottle traveled almost eight feet into the crib without their help? Was the lady Cliff had seen in the room caring for their son? From that time they had no concern about the cold spots in that room or the occasional sound of footsteps in other parts of the house. If they had a friendly spirit in their house, she was welcome to stay.

* Children understand

Their second child was about two years old when Cliff was working afternoon shifts. He would be home during the day with their young sons, while their mother was at work. Each day, Cliff put his youngest son in his crib for an afternoon nap. Contented chattering preceded falling asleep. One day the chattering would not end. Cliff swung the door almost closed to make the bedroom quieter to help his son fall asleep. Soon the chattering increased. Cliff went to rock his son asleep. As Cliff opened the door, he saw his son standing inside the crib facing the door. The toddler looked up startled and told his father: "You scared the lady away." At first Cliff felt a chill up and down his spine. Then the memories of the baby bottle and the vanishing lady came back. He felt reassured that any spirit here was caring and protective.

* "Remember when I was the daddy and you were the little boy?"

Cliff's son asked him this question at age three. Cliff was paying attention to something else and did not want to be bothered just then. However, his son was insistent. He tugged at Cliff's sleeve to get his attention. "Daddy, remember when you were the little boy and I was the daddy?" Cliff replied with partial attention. "Sure I remember when I was a little boy, just like you are now."

"No." He insisted, pulling harder on Cliff's arm to make him listen. "When I was the daddy and you were the little boy?" Cliff turned to listen to the childish fantasy. "Tell me about it, son." *(His son's enthusiastic chatter is edited for clarity.)* "Remember when we were riding in the back of a truck. There was all our furniture in the truck and you and I were riding in the back with all the furniture and the truck was moving along the road. You kept climbing up the sides of the truck to look over and see what was outside." His son had Cliff's full attention now. He was listening intently to every word with chills running up and down his spine. Long-lost memories were flooding Cliff's mind.

"Because I was afraid that you would fall, I kept pulling you back down to safety. Then you would just start to climb up again. Finally I got your tricycle down from the stack of furniture and I cleared a spot for you to ride it. I was afraid you would fall off the truck."

This was amazing. How could his son have known about this? The move into Toronto 30 years before his birth? It had happened when Cliff was only four. His father was moving his family to a house much closer to a new job in Toronto. The owner of a coal company was a friend of his father and had lent him a truck for the move. His mother and sister rode in the front with the driver. He and his father were in the back of the open vehicle. He was everywhere at once. It seemed like a good idea to climb up on the sideboards of the truck to watch the land flash by. He made several attempts but his father pulled him down each time. Then a new approach. His father let him burn off his energy and excitement by riding his tricycle in the tiny clearing amid the furniture.

Cliff had never thought of it since or told anyone about it. Three years after the move, his father had passed away. How, then, could his son know about this? Was it genetic memory, an inner knowledge passed on from one generation to another? Another possibility was telepathic communication. It may be that information is just picked out of the air when a person is in the proper frame of mind and is open to receptivity. A third possibility was reincarnation. Could Cliff's son possibly also have been his father? As Cliff learned more about reincarnation, he decided that this is not such a remote possibility.

* Psychic research lawyers

Shortly after a deep-trance channeling session at a psychic fair at the Toronto International Centre, a private detective telephoned from Toronto asking whether Cliff would perform a channeling session for the Society for Psychic Research. His officiousness suggested that he was impressed by the credentials of those who would witness the session. He stressed repeatedly that Cliff and Linda not be late. Upon arrival, they were met by a group of lawyers, wives and girlfriends, who seemed ready to disprove the session. One young observer used crude language to tell Cliff that none of them believed in this nonsense. Cliff and Linda explained what would happen before Cliff entered trance. Each observer could ask one question in turn. The session would likely end by 9 p.m. However during the evening, disbelief became curiosity. Questions and discussions after the trance session kept the Prestons until 1 a.m. A chance encounter with the detective a year later revealed that the answer to a question asked of The Echo was later proven true. The female questioner who worked in a bank had asked the amount of her cash at closing the following Friday evening. The answer was a figure such as $3,372.64. However, the questioner was not on cash the following Friday. Another teller took the balance for that window. $3,732.64. The individual numbers were the same. The two middle figures had been transposed.

* Ghost warrior

It is believed that sometime during the late 1600s, Iroquois swept over the Niagara River from New York State and massacred a gathering of many other different tribes at the head of the river, the site of the present-day town of Fort Erie. One of the archeological digs in the late 1960s and early 1970s in the Bridgeburg section of the town took an entire summer. Members of the Fort Erie Underwater Recovery Team provided 24-hour security as the Royal Ontario Museum worked at the site. One day workers who had assembled bones from human skeletons on an adjacent sidewalk for further study were called away briefly.

Immediately, a car appeared, a woman emerged, and placed the bones in the trunk. Cliff and the other volunteer security staff assumed she was a member of the team. Later they learned that the woman was not associated with the museum. To Cliff's knowledge, the woman was never apprehended nor the bones recovered.

One night in 1977, Cliff was sleeping in his rented three-level unit of the apartment building that had been converted from the Bridgeburg school. He was awakened by a loud rustling and scraping sound. Dazedly he looked around the room. There was a slight movement on the far side. A shadowy flicker turned into the form of a man. Shocked, Cliff sat up in bed. He was looking at an Indian in full war dress. Feathers protruded from his hair above flashes of red, white and black paint on his face. He wore breech clout and moccasins. He seemed to carry a club in his hands, held protectively in front, as if he expected an attack. Cliff was transfixed as he absorbed the spectacle.

The warrior began to move slowly and stealthily across the room, past the foot of the bed. His moccasins continued to scrape the floor as he searched cautiously for safe footing. Another flicker of movement in the shadows, behind the first warrior, brought a second, and a third. The two new warriors were covered in war paint and similarly clad. Cliff's mind raced. Who were these men? How could they get through solid brick walls? Cliff realized that he felt no fear. The visitors did not seem to see him. Then they disappeared through the brick wall of the second-floor bedroom. It seemed that Cliff had witnessed a ghostly re-enactment of a past event. The warriors appeared again occasionally over the next few months, acting as they had the first time. The sound would awake Cliff again, but he was no longer surprised or concerned. He had reason to move after these months of sightings and wonders whether the warriors appeared to subsequent occupants.

* Old John

Cliff and his first wife had a quiet, industrious neighbor aged about 80 who lived alone and mostly kept to himself. They called him John as they had never heard his name. There did not seem to be any family members to visit Old John. He seemed content on his own, regularly working on his property and gardens. A pleasant young couple with two small sons heard that he had extra space in his house and asked whether they could rent if from him. He agreed to rent the top floor of the bungalow and move to the basement. Within a week, the couple changed. The small boys were directed to stomp on John's beautiful gardens, reducing them to waste. Nightly and throughout weekends, the couple drank. They fought viciously, often ripping doors from the hinges and breaking windows. They attacked each other with any nearby object. Once a hammer was used. Neighbors sometimes called police to stop the drunken brawls between the adults, who would then vocally abuse the attending officers, daring them to step onto the property and threatening to sue them if they did. When John backed his vintage 1936 Oldsmobile out of the garage, the woman extended a broom-handle or mop-handle out of the broken kitchen window against the garage door. This created scratches and dents on the car. Old John gave up trying to move his car and began walking to his destinations.

Finally, a vicious dog was tied at the top of the cellar stairs in an effort to keep John from leaving the house. He crawled out the cellar window and went to Cliff's house for help.

The local MP and sheriff's office became involved. After a series of warnings, the couple were locked out of the house by the sheriff. Although they were evicted, it was after major damage had been done to the house. Most of the windows were broken. Pet rabbits had made a mess of the kitchen. The SPCA was called to remove the vicious dog, which was actually starving.

A few days after the eviction, Old John was lying on Cliff's front steps in a fetal position. He had crawled there since he was too weak to stand. Cliff lifted him into his car and took him to the hospital. He could not be admitted because he had no family doctor. A nurse arranged by telephone that Cliff take him to a doctor's office. Cliff carried the crumpled old man past the waiting patients into the examination room. One look at the limp form and the doctor asked whether Cliff could return the "very ill" man to hospital. The doctor phoned ahead so the second greeting at the hospital was cordial. A wheelchair appeared. John was wheeled away as Cliff said he would visit in the morning.

"No come, I no be here," was the reply in a strong European accent. It was 4 p.m. Cliff was already late for work. Approximately 9 p.m. he received a call from his wife. "The hospital just called. John has passed away."

Several years later, their first son, during his pre-school years, would often describe the face of a kindly old man smiling at him from a spot near the ceiling, in the corner of the kitchen. Their son said that the man called himself Old John. Their son was born well after John's passing and had never heard of him. How could he have known to call his vision Old John? Was the kindly old man gratefully watching over the friendly family?

* Rescuer in a black suit

Cliff was working a second job as a waiter in the old Queen's Hotel in Fort Erie in 1966. One autumn Saturday afternoon a young boy burst into the rear-empty beverage room, shouting that his friend had just fallen over the concrete retaining wall into the swift current of the Niagara River. Cliff and several patrons ran across the road to the empty park. They saw a small boy, shivering and dripping on the grass, 3 m (10 feet) from the retaining wall. The top of the continuous wall is 3 m (10 feet) above the surface of the rapidly moving water. There are no steps or ladders to escape from the river. They asked how the seven-or-eight-year-old boy had reached safety? He said that he was in the water and that a man in a black suit reached over the wall and lifted him to the spot where he was standing. The man had then left in the direction of the river. The view from the hotel was unobstructed and it would take someone several minutes to get out of sight. Yet no one had seen the rescuer. The facts could not be challenged. What were the reasonable explanations? Was spiritual intervention possible?

* A voice from beyond

A friend of Cliff's in the 1970s married a popular man. For several weeks the couple seemed blissful. However, Bill, the husband, began suffering from persistent flu. After unsuccessful medication, tests were done. The diagnosis changed to advanced leukemia. Prognosis terminal. He underwent three months of harsh chemotherapy. When Cliff saw him next, he was a walking skeleton. Although Bill needed to talk to someone about his situation, the dying man's family and friends would not talk openly about his impending death.

Cliff's reputation for spiritual and mystical interests drew Bill. During the fourth month of the illness, they talked about spirits, religions, reincarnation and anything else that seemed relevant. They searched for answers together. They talked about many things and always returned to death, the most difficult subject of all. Of the many words that they exchanged, Cliff remembers most clearly Bill's comment during a visit home from the hospital. "You are the only person who will openly discuss death with me. I know that I am dying and I thank you for helping me to settle my mind."

Bill passed into Spirit quietly and peacefully, less than six months after his marriage. He chose to be alone at the time, having told his wife to leave his bedside long enough to have a meal. He wanted to save her the pain of seeing her loved one die. Cliff visited the funeral home early, before family and friends. There was no one around, as Cliff approached the casket. He saw a smiling photograph of Bill and smelled the perfume of the flowers. He looked at the photo and placed a hand on the casket, for some reason saying aloud: "Bill, now do you understand what I was trying to tell you about life continuing in Spirit?" Suddenly, from all around Cliff, from the walls, from everywhere at once, a peaceful voice resounded.

"Yes, now I know."

Cliff lurched back from the coffin in surprise. There was no one else in the room to speak.

"Yes, now I know."

One brief reassuring statement from everywhere and nowhere. It fortified Cliff's belief in the soul's immortality more than any reading or preaching could ever have done.

* An astral adventure

One night after Cliff had gone to sleep as usual, he had a strange sensation of hurtling through darkness. Then there was flat land below, bathed in beautiful, brilliant sunshine as far as he could see. Then a wide, quiet river came into view. Flying over the river, he saw two figures in dark clothing on the far shore. They seemed expectant. Cliff was losing altitude as he drew near. They were dressed in long, dark, hooded robes much like medieval monks. A pale blue shimmering light danced in and around their hoods, obscuring their faces. Cliff landed cautiously. He sensed that they were welcoming him. His concerns vanished as he accepted each extended hand. The faces of his maternal grandparents replaced the shimmering light as contact was made. They radiated perfect peace and health, appearing much younger than Cliff had ever known them. Yet he knew them immediately. They walked hand-in-hand away from the river, along a path bordered by yellow flowers. They communicated telepathically in this beautiful land of clear blue sky, sunshine, flowers and a path disappearing into the horizon. They said that death is not to be feared or mourned. It is just a change of form, one step forward in the soul's search for perfection. He knew that his grandparents were extremely happy and would one day decide to return to the earth plane for further life experiences.

They returned to the shore. Each grandparent kissed Cliff's cheek lovingly and released his hand. Suddenly he was airborne again. Rapidly he rose over the river and re-entered the darkness, hurtling through the black void. Suddenly, he was wide awake, lying on his back in bed. He felt powerless to move his limbs. His entire body was experiencing a "pins and needles" sensation. Many minutes passed before he could regain control of his body and move.

Cliff remembers the feeling of warmth and the texture of the skin of his grandparents' hands, exceptionally clearly. He also remembers the warm sun on his face and the powerful, fulfilling love he received. The physical sensations were real. They have been indelibly impressed in his memory.

* Premonition

When Cliff was a stationary engineer with the Northwest Territories government in Rankin Inlet, he acted as liaison for a project in which commercial divers inspected underwater piping extending 1.6 km (1 mile) out from shore under the sea.

He spent a lot of time in a small boat observing the young divers and recording the operation. It was an exhilarating experience for Cliff. He realized that he could use all his years of diving experience again by passing on his knowledge to other young divers.

In 1992 he registered for a diving instructor training program in the Florida Keys. He booked leave requests, vacation time, air travel and accommodation several months in advance.

He flew out of Rankin Inlet at -30° C (-22° F). After an overnight stop in Toronto, he flew to Miami where the temperature was more than 34° C (90° F). Compared to the cold, fresh air of the Arctic, the air here smelled stale and sour. One more flight, to Marathon in the Keys, and Cliff would realize his dream of teaching scuba diving.

The first day of training was spent in review work, practising basic pool skills and getting to know the other instructors and the students. Each participant was pool-tested to be sure that he was physically fit and qualified to continue safely with the training. They would be taken to an ocean reef the next day.

Cliff was elated. He would be diving on a coral reef for the first time since his navy days, 25 years ago. He had dived throughout the Caribbean Islands then. This was wonderful.

But then the dream came.

In his dream, he saw the diving boat, near the reef, tossing wildly on an angry sea. He saw frantic activity among the persons on board. There was a sense of panic. Dark clouds raced overhead, obliterating the sun. Wind and rain lashed the tiny vessel, yet there was no move to run before the storm. Everyone was peering over the side in awed expectation. The heads of divers popped through the surface of the water. They were carefully holding something.

The dream scene shifted to a better view of the object that the divers were holding.

They were holding Cliff.

He was lifeless His face had the familiar blue tinge of drowning victims.

Cliff had drowned. He was the obje ct of a recovery search. He was dead.

He awakened with a fearful start. He was standing in the middle of the hotel room floor.

It was only a dream. Thank God.

The dream was so upsetting that Cliff cancelled his training in the morning. He has never dived since that horrible dream.

He knows that he could have toughed it out and completed the course. He knows that he could have been "macho."

He also knows that later that same morning, the Florida Keys were suddenly struck by a hurricane that lasted for the next two days. All boats in the area were ordered to the safety of port.

****   PART 2   ****

The Echo

Original transcripts of channeling sessions

The following transcripts are from deep-trance channeling sessions of The Echo by Cliff Preston. The transcripts appear as originally written, with minor editing for clarity and consistency.

The transcripts are presented in general chronological and progressive order, starting from 1982 and ending with the two sessions over the Mitchell-Hedges Crystal Skull in February, 1996. Most of these transcripts are exclusive, appearing in print for the first time.

The Echo's Code of Living and Other Statements are presented at the end of this section.

Chapter 6   Introduction to the The Echo

This is a transcript of a channeling session with The Echo, who speak through Cliff Preston while he is in a specific altered state of consciousness, termed deep trance. Cliff is not consciously aware of the material being given during the sessions.

Linda Preston is the trance director for all sessions.

We join the session, at the final stage of the trance induction.

DIR: Please clear the mind. Indicate when the mind is clear.

ECHO: INDEED SO.

DIR: Please locate and assimilate with the form of your director.

ECHO: INDEED. FORM FOUND. ASSIMILATION COMPLETE.

DIR: Is all well with the form Clifford?

ECHO: INDEED. THE FORM OF THE ONE CLIFFORD, TRANCE STATE E, LEVEL 927 BROADENING NATURALLY

DIR: Thank You. May we proceed with questions?

ECHO: INDEED. WE WILL ASSIST TO THE UTMOST OF OUR ABILITY.

DIR: Echo, we are going to do an interview of you, and first...

ECHO: INDEED. WE ARE HIGHLY HONOURED.

DIR: .... Would you please tell us who you are?

ECHO: INDEED. WE ARE THE ECHO, AS THE NAME ECHO BE PRESENTED BY THAT OF THE FORM OF THE ONE CLIFFORD. WE BE THAT OF A SPIRITUAL ASSISTANCE TO THOSE IN THE PHYSICAL REALM.

DIR: Can you tell us then, what you are as well?

ECHO: INDEED. HERE, WE, THE ECHO, BE NUMBERING PRESENTLY THAT OF 10,242 OF DISCARNATE BEINGS. WE BE IN THE DISCARNATE OR SPIRITUAL FORM HERE, WHICH BE THAT, MERELY, OF THE THOUGHT PATTERN OF THAT REFER "ENERGY SOURCES. WE OF THE ECHO BE FLUCTUATING IN NUMBERS, AND INDEED ACCORDING TO THAT LEVEL OF QUERY HERE.

DIR: Can you tell us how many entities you have access to?

ECHO: THAT OF THE ACCESS TO ENTITY, HERE BE NUMBERING BEYOND THAT   REFER "COUNTABLE".

DIR: Why do you speak to us through deep trance?

ECHO: INDEED. WHY NOT? YOU ARE INDEED NICE PEOPLE!

90

UNDERSTAND HERE: IN REALITY, IT BE THAT OF THE MATTER OF ASSISTANCE TO THOSE IN THE PHYSICAL REALM. ALSO HERE, THERE BE THAT OF THE SELFISH REASONS. IT BE THAT OF ASSISTANCE TO WE, THE ECHO, IN THAT IN ASSISTING OTHERS WE ALSO ASSIST OURSELVES IN GROWTH AND LEARNING FORMAT.

DIR: In what areas then, do you hope to assist us?

ECHO: INDEED. IN THAT OF AREA OF ASSISTANCE HERE, WE OFFER SOME DEGREE OF THE UNDERSTANDING OF THAT REFER SPIRITUALITY. WE OFFER HERE SOME DEGREE OF THE UNDERSTANDING OF THE ˉSELVES", YOUR REFERENCE, "THOSE IN THE PHYSICAL REALM", OFFER UNDERSTANDING OF THE WORKINGS OF THE PHYSICAL BODY AND INDEED OF THE MIND OF THOSE INVOLVED IN THE PHYSICAL.

DIR: How and in what areas do you assist yourselves by this communication?

ECHO: INDEED. THERE BE HERE MERELY THAT OF THE ACT OF ASSISTANCE TO   THOSE IN THE PHYSICAL BE IN A MANNER OF ASSISTANCE TO WE, THE   ECHO, IN THAT WE GAIN UNDERSTANDING ALSO HERE. IN THAT THROUGH ASSISTANCE OF OTHERS, WE, THEN, IN EFFECT HERE, GAIN POINTS, AS IT WERE, IN YOUR UNDERSTANDING.

DIR: Have you ever lived before, and the other entities in the group?

ECHO: INDEED SO UNDERSTAND: AS PREVIOUSLY STATED, THAT OF THE SPOKES ENTITY HERE BE THAT OF GOLUDE OF EXISTENCE THAT REFER "ATLANTEAN" TIMES, IN TEACHINGS AND DEALINGS OF THE WORKING OF THE MIND OF THE HUMAN ANIMAL. OTHERS BE IN THE DEALINGS OF THE PHYSICAL BODY. OTHERS THERE BE IN THE DEALINGS OF THE MANUAL LABOURS, ETC., ETC.

DIR: When somebody asks you a question, if you yourself, as Golude, do not know the answer, how then do you get that other information? Are you blended into one person for deep trance sessions?

ECHO: INDEED. UNDERSTAND: IN THAT OF THE FORM OF THE ONE CLIFFORD ALLOWING THE OPENING OF THE MIND TO, IN EFFECT, TUNE TO THAT REFER "DEEP TRANCE STATE", AND IN SO DOING TUNE TO THAT REALM IN WHICH KNOWLEDGES BE AVAILABLE. WHEN THE QUESTION BE PRESENTED, THEN WE, OF THE ECHO, IN OUR REFERENCE HERE "CONCENTRATION GROUP MIND CONCEPT" HERE. WE THEN FEED, FILTER THROUGH THE MIND OF THE FORM CLIFFORD THOSE INFORMATIONS THAT BE AVAILABLE PRESENTLY IN RELATION OF THE QUERY.

DIR: Now I feel as though you don't actually enter the body I am assuming that, from what you have just said. How then do you manipulate the tiny voice box?

ECHO: INDEED. UNDERSTAND HERE: IT BE THAT WITHIN THAT REFER "BRAIN COMPLEX" OF THE ANIMAL MAN, THERE BE HERE AREAS THAT MAY BE ELECTRICALLY STIMULATED.

HERE UNDERSTAND: SPEAKING OF "ELECTRICALLY", WE DO NOT REFER TO THAT OF THE 120 VOLT CHARGES HERE. RATHER THIS BE APPLIED MENTALLY AND THAT OF THE ELECTRICAL IMPULSE BE OF MICRO-MINI VOLTAGES. THAT OF THOSE IN EXISTENCE IN THE PHYSICAL HAVE NOT AS YET ATTAINED THE TECHNOLOGY HERE, IN THE MEASUREMENT THEREOF.

DIR: In our scientific circles, Echo, researchers would hook up a person with EEG apparatus, Electro-encephalogram. Are you familiar with this device?

ECHO: INDEED SO.

DIR: What would this apparatus show in Clifford's trance state.

ECHO: INDEED. IN THE FORM OF THE ONE CLIFFORD IT WILL SHOW HIGH DEGREE OF BRAIN ACTIVITIES, HIGH DEGREE OF TENSIONS THROUGHOUT THE PHYSICAL BEING. BEYOND THIS, BE LITTLE IN THE VIEWING.

DIR: Will this be a typical pattern, usually related to sleep?

ECHO: INDEED. SOMEWHAT. HOWEVER, DO UNDERSTAND: EACH ENTITY IN THE PERFORMANCE OF THAT REFER "DEEP TRANCE" WILL INDEED REGISTER SOMEWHAT DIFFERENTLY.

DIR: Is there any similarity between Deep Trance phenomena and when one is actually out of body at night in the sleep state?

ECHO: INDEED. THERE BE SIMILARITIES TO THAT OF THE REMAINING BODY, INDEED SO.

DIR: Could you explain what the Akashic Records are and how much access you have to these records?

ECHO: INDEED. THAT REFER "THE AKASHIC BOOK OF LIFE" OR "BOOK OF THE DEAD". THERE BE MANY TERMS OF THE SAME SOURCE. HERE UNDERSTAND THAT EACH OCCURRENCE, EACH THOUGHT, EACH ACTIVITY ON THAT OF REFERENCE PLANET EARTH BE COMMITTED TO THE ATMOSPHERE AND REMAIN MUCH AS IN REFERENCE AS THE "ENCIRCLEMENT" THAT BE VIEWED ABOUT THAT OF THE PLANET SATURN. HERE UNDERSTAND: THIS BE INVISIBLE, IMMEASURABLE.
HOWEVER, IN THE TUNING OF THE MIND, AS PREVIOUSLY STATED, WE MAY THEN OFFER SOME KNOWLEDGE FROM THAT REFER "AKASHIC RECORD". IN REFERENCE THAT OF THE AMOUNT OF AVAILABILITY HERE, THERE BE THAT WE, THE ECHO, VIEW INFORMATIONS REQUESTED AS THOUGH VIEWING A SIGNPOST IN A SWIRLING FOG. AT ONE SECOND IN TIME THE SIGN BE CLEAR AND LEGIBLE. AT THE NEXT SECOND IN TIME, IT BE COVERED, PARTIALLY OR TOTALLY BY THAT REFER "SWIRLING FOG". THIS BE REASON WHY, WHEN AN ENTITY QUERY ONE SOURCE, ONE INFORMATION BE PRESENTED, AND IN THAT OF THE QUERY PRESENTED TO ANOTHER SOURCE, THERE BE SOMEWHAT DIFFERENCE.

DIR: Can you exist within or outside of time?

ECHO: INDEED: THERE BE NO SUCH FACTOR AS TIME IN YOUR EXISTENCE OR IN OUR EXISTENCE.

DIR: It is illusionary then?

ECHO: INDEED. ABSTRACT AND ILLUSIONARY.

DIR: Can you actually manipulate time through your space or utilize it?

ECHO: INDEED. THE ENTITIES PRESENT BE AWARE OF MANIPULATIONS IN THAT OF THE STOPPING OF RECORDING DEVICES, THAT OF THE BLANKING OF RECORDING UPON RECORDING DEVICES ETC.

DIR: Obviously a great deal of what we call electromagnetic energy call be manipulated from your side of existence. Is this correct?

ECHO: INDEED SO. UNDERSTAND: ALL THINGS: AIR, IONOSPHERE, WATER, EARTH, ALL THINGS BE ELECTROMAGNETIC IN BASIS. UNDERSTAND: HE, WHO FIRST DISCOVERS A SECRET OF MAGNETICS AND ELECTRICS WILL THEN HAVE ACCESS TO USAGES, PERFORMANCES, THAT BE BEYOND THAT OF PRESENT UNDERSTANDING OF THE ANIMAL MAN.

DIR: Can researchers discuss these types of things with you, The Echo, and get closer to beneficial truths and utilization of these energies?

ECHO: INDEED. UNDERSTAND HERE: WE MAY DISCUSS HERE ONLY TO THAT OF THE: VOCABULARY USAGE OF THE ENTITY IN PERFORMANCE OF THE TRANCE STATE. WE HAVE AVAILABILITY OF SOME KNOWLEDGES

BEYOND THE KNOWLEDGE OF THE PERFORMER OF THE TRANCE STATE. HOWEVER, THAT OF REFERENCE HERE "TECHNICAL" LANGUAGES BE BEYOND THE SCOPE OF WE, THE ECHO, IN ASSOCIATION OF THE FORM OF THE ONE CLIFFORD, AT PRESENT.

DIR: Can this be changed?

ECHO: INDEED SO.

DIR: How?

ECHO: INDEED. THROUGH THAT OF THE FORM OF THE ONE CLIFFORD BECOMING FAMILIAR IN THAT OF THE USAGE OF THE TECHNICAL TERMS.

DIR: Will he have to memorize these things or would he be able to read a book and you could have access to that?

ECHO: INDEED. THERE BE HERE ONLY REQUIREMENT OF THE INPUT. WE DO NOT ASK THAT THE ENTITY BECOME, REFERENCE HERE, "RHODES SCHOLAR".

DIR: In other words, input to the subconscious mind will quite suffice?

ECHO: INDEED SO.

DIR: Have you spoken to others in the past?

ECHO: INDEED. WE AND/OR PART OF WE INDEED HAVE SPOKEN IN THAT REFER "PAST" USING OTHER ENTITIES.

DIR: Have you then spoken through people in the past that we, ourselves might know, like famous persons?

ECHO: INDEED. BE HERE THAT OF APPROXIMATE 1200 YEARS PRIOR THAT OF THE PRESENT CALENDAR USAGE. THERE BE HERE ONE REFER "ERICTEVAS", THERE BE ONE REFER "NOSTRADAMUS", THERE BE MANY OF OTHERS THROUGHOUT THAT REFER HISTORY. THERE BE THAT REFER "JACKSON", THERE BE THAT REFER "DICKENS", THERE BE THAT REFER "CAYCE", THERE BE THOSE OF THE PRESENT PHYSICAL RESONANCE HERE ALSO.

DIR: That would be persons whom we know, such as Doug Cottrell, Ian Borts, Serge Grandbois?

ECHO: INDEED SO. PETERSON *[Author's note: Ross Peterson in Michigan.]*-- INDEED. THERE BE MANY THAT ATTAIN CONTACT OF THE --REFERENCE HERE-- "SOURCE". THIS BE UNDERSTOOD, THAT THERE IT BE NOT NECESSARILY THAT OF SPECIFIC GROUPING AS WE REFER "WE THE ECHO", RATHER THAT OF WHICH WE, THE ECHO, BE A PART OF.

DIR: How many Deep Trance Psychics are there at present throughout the world?

ECHO: INDEED. THOSE IN ACTUALITY OF PERFORMANCE APPROXIMATE HERE 700.

DIR: You mentioned the name "Nostradamus". So this information, his predictions, that type of thing, was actually given in a Deep Trance State?

ECHO: INDEED. REFERENCE "GIVEN" HERE. BE THAT OF RATHER "DEVELOPED". UNDERSTAND: IT BE HERE NOT THAT OF DEEP TRANCE STATE, RATHER THAT REFER "MOBILE TRANCE STATE".

97

DIR: And you also mentioned Dickens. Some of the stories that he wrote where you as the larger grouping, were part of, actually helped channel that information through Dickens?

ECHO: INDEED SO.

DIR: Such as the famous story he wrote, called "A Christmas Carol"?

ECHO: INDEED SO. THERE BE HERE PRESENTATION OF THOSE DESIRED IDEAS.

DIR: So you are communicating not only through Deep Trance, but through other means, such as Automatic Writing and Animated Trance.

ECHO: INDEED SO.

DIR: Echo, Dickens was said to have experienced Cosmic Consciousness?

ECHO: INDEED SO.

DIR: How many entities are there within this larger grouping that you are part of, that speak through Deep Trance Psychics?

ECHO: INDEED. UNDERSTAND HERE: AS PREVIOUS STATED HERE, THESE BE UNCOUNTABLE. UNDERSTAND: ALL THAT DESIRE ASSISTANCE, FIND ASSISTANCE AVAILABLE THROUGH THAT REFER "CONTACT" OF SUCH AS WE, THE ECHO, AND INDEED THE AKASHIC RECORDS. ALL HAVE AVAILABILITY HERE.

DIR: Echo, does it take a certain amount of practice, when an entity spokesman for the group starts speaking through a Group Trance Psychic? Does it take practice on the part of the spokes-person?

ECHO: INDEED SO. UNDERSTAND WE, ALTHOUGH PERFECT IN EVERY MANNER, ALSO THE PHYSICAL ENTITY BE PERFECT IN EVERY MANNER, DO REQUIRE TRAININGS.

(laughter by those interviewing The Echo)

DIR: Biblical literature refers to the term "Angels". Are you what is considered "Angels"?

ECHO: INDEED SO. UNDERSTAND: ANGELS BE IN REALITY ASSISTANTS TO THOSE IN THE PHYSICAL REALM AND INDEED NOT A HIGHER OR LOWER BEINGS. MERELY BEINGS EXISTING WITHIN A SOMEWHAT PARALLEL REALM, UNDERSTAND: WE DO NOT GROW FEATHERS FROM OUR BACKS.

DIR: Where did that expression come from?

ECHO: INDEED. UNDERSTAND: THAT OF THE VISUALIZING OF A SPIRITUAL ENTITY: OFTTIMES IT APPEAR THAT OF THE SPIRITUAL ENTITY BE IN POSITION NOT OF CONTACT WITH GROUND, FLOOR OR OTHER STRUCTURES. IT APPEAR AS THE ENTITY BE FLOATING TO ONE IN THE PHYSICAL REALM. IN THIS UNDERSTANDING, THEN, UNDERSTAND THAT THOSE PRESENTING THE IDEA OF A BEING VIEWED FLOATING, IN ORDER THAT THIS BE ACCEPTED AND THOSE ENTITY EXPLAINING, BE NOT STONED TO DEATH, THERE BE PRESENTATION OF WINGS HERE.

99

DIR: Pretty logical.
Is any of the literature that we know of, like the Bible and other standard spiritual type literature, is that a direct result of what we know as Deep Trance?

ECHO: INDEED. PORTIONS THEREOF.

DIR: Could you please give some examples?

ECHO: INDEED. THAT OF THE DICTUM RELATED TO BEGINNINGS, SUCH AS THE ADAM AND EVE TALE. THIS BE PRESENTED TO MAN IN ORDER THAT HE MAY HAVE SOME UNDERSTANDINGS, IN SYMBOLOGY, OF THESE BEGINNINGS.
THAT OF THE KORAN BE PRESENTED IN NEAR ENTIRETY IN STATE OF TRANCE. THAT OF REFERENCE HERE "SEPHER YETZERA" BE DICTATED IN STATE OF TRANCE. THAT OF HIGH DEGREE OF CONTENTS OF THAT REFER "KABBALA" BE DICTATED IN A STATE OF TRANCE.
UNDERSTAND: THAT OF REFERENCE HERE "DEEP TRANCE STATE" BE NOT BY ANY MEANS DUE TO ANIMAL MAN. THIS BE AN INHERENT TALENT AND A TALENT THAT BE PRACTICED FROM TIME IMMEMORIAL.

DIR: What about some of the eastern literature, like the "VEDAS"?

ECHO: INDEED SO. UNDERSTAND: THESE ALSO. THERE BE LITERATURES IN ALL PORTIONS OF THE PLANET EARTH THAT BE DICTATED FROM WITHIN A STATE OF TRANCE.

DIR: Did the high priests practice deep trance?

100

ECHO: INDEED SO. IT BE STATED: "MEDITATIVE STATE".

DIR: When some of the characters we are most familiar with, like in the Bible, when they talk   to God, was that like us talking to you?

ECHO: INDEED, SOMEWHAT. IN THAT OF REFERENCE HERE "MOSES", THIS ENTITY, IN FORMAT OF FASTING THAT OF APPROXIMATE HERE 12 DAYS, TO RECEIVE PHYSICALLY, IMPRESSION, VISIONS THAT FORETOLD TO THIS ENTITY THAT OF THE NEED OF A FORMAT OF THE RULES, LAWS, THAT WILL ASSIST HIS PEOPLE IN FURTHER DEVELOPMENT. THIS THEN BE PRESENTED IN THE FORMAT OF DISCUSSION WITH THAT WHICH THE ENTITY PERCEIVE AS GOD, AND THERE BE HERE BORN THAT REFER "THE COMMANDMENTS".

DIR: So when Moses went to the mountain, did he receive the information inspirationally, and then he carved the tablets?

ECHO: INDEED SO. UNDERSTAND: THERE BE PRESENTED TO THAT OF TRIBE THAT THESE TABLETS BE HANDED BY THE HAND OF GOD, IN ORDER THAT CREDENCE BE ADDED HERE.

DIR: That means that reasonable common sense was not quite good enough to convince the people?

ECHO: INDEED SO. UNDERSTAND:

(trance state J, level 7721, maintaining)

101

THE ENTITIES IN THAT OF THE PRESENT BE IN REALIZATION OF THE SENSE OF SUPERSTITIONS THAT EXIST WITHIN THAT OF THE FRAME OF EXISTENCE OF THAT REFER "MOSES". THIS ENTITY BE IN REALITY THAT REFER "MAGUS" AND PRESENT TO ITS PEOPLE A STONE TABLET, STATING RULES OF EXISTENCE. THESE PEOPLE THEN SAY, FEEL, THIS BE "ONLY OLD MOSES ATTEMPTING TO JUSTIFY HIS EXISTENCE AMONG US". RATHER HERE THE ENTITY MOSES APPROACH WITH FIRE IN EYE, STONE IN HAND AND STATE THIS BE A REVELATION FROM THAT OF THE GREAT ALL, AND IN THIS MANNER IT EXPLAIN THERE BE OCCURRENCE OF VOICES FROM HEAVEN AND CREDENCE THEN BE PRESENT.

DIR: Very interesting. Our standard religious movements of today consider what we are doing right now, I.E. this interview, to be totally incredible, bad, satanistic, not to be done, communicating with the dead, and a thousand other things. Could you perhaps enlighten us here?

ECHO: INDEED SO. UNDERSTAND: IN ANY RELIGION, IN ANY PORTION OF THE PLANET EARTH, THERE BE A COMMON FACTOR IN RELIGIONS. THIS BE A SENSE OF RESTRICTIVENESS, OF NEEDS OF CONTROL OF THE FOLLOWERS OF ITS RELIGION. IN THAT OF THE REFERENCE HERE, "SQUELCHING" OF THE FREEDOM OF FREE THOUGHT, THESE RELIGIONS THEN MAINTAIN AND EVEN BUILD FOLLOWERS IN NUMBER.
UNDERSTAND THEN: THESE ENTITIES DEALING IN RELIGIONS BE IN REALITY DEALING IN NUMBERS, RATHER THAN SPIRITUALISTIC GROWTH AMONG THE MEMBERS. IN THE

PLACING OF RESTRICTIONS, THE FREEDOMS ALSO BE LIMITED, AND THOSE ACCEPTING THESE RESTRICTIONS CARRY ON IN THEIR EXISTENCES IN THAT STATE REFER "IGNORANCE".
UNDERSTAND: THE SQUELCHING, THE HOLDING DOWN OF INFORMATIONS BE PRIMARY METHOD IN THE CONTROL AND DIRECTION OF ANY POPULACE.

DIR: So with all that in mind, what philosophy would you The Echo present to be of most benefit to mankind?

ECHO: INDEED. THE PHILOSOPHY HERE BE SIMPLE AND STRAIGHTFORWARD:

FOLLOW THE DICTATES OF YOUR HEART IN CONJUNCTION WITH THE SENSE AND REASONABLENESS OF YOUR MIND. IN THE FOLLOWING OF ANOTHER, YOU ARE RELINQUISHING THE FREEDOM OF YOUR THOUGHTS.

DIR: That simple?

ECHO: INDEED SO.

DIR: Thanks. I have a question about CLIFF right now. What happens to CLIFF during Deep Trance and why is it that he has no recall of anything?

ECHO: LITTLE OCCUR TO THE ENTITY DURING THAT OF THE STATE REFER "TRANCE". IT BE MERELY THAT OF THE REMOVAL OF THE CONSCIOUSNESS OF THE ENTITY IN ORDER THAT SUCH AS WE, THE ECHO, MAY THEN USE THE FORM. THIS BE DONE IN TOTAL

AGREEMENT WITH THE FORM AND IN THE UNDERSTANDING THAT THERE CAN BE NO HARM TO THE FORM.

IN THAT OF OCCURRENCE, IT BE THAT OF THE MIND FORMAT OF THE ENTITY INDEED REMAIN WITHIN THE ENTITY, BE MERELY BLOCKED DUE TO THE ENERGIES THAT NEEDS BE HERE APPLIED BY WE THE ECHO. THIS BE REASONINGS OF THAT OF LACK OF MEMORIES HERE.

DIR: Do you give him information of another sort, while he is in this state of consciousness?

ECHO: INDEED. SOMEWHAT. THERE BE HERE A GROWING UNDERSTANDING DEVELOPING WITHIN THE FORM OF THE ONE CLIFFORD. THIS BE IN EFFECT A SIDE EFFECT OF THE TRANCE STATE. THE FORM, YOU WILL DISCOVER, THERE BE APPROACHING LIFE, APPROACHING RELATIONSHIPS, APPROACHING OTHER ENTITIES IN THE PHYSICAL REALM WITH MORE UNDERSTANDING AND INDEED WITH LESS ACCEPTANCE OF RESPONSIBILITY FOR OTHERS.

DIR: Did you say then, performing the Deep Trance, a person can grow faster, or can a person grow equally as fast, not performing Trance?

ECHO: INDEED. IN THAT OF THE PERFORMANCE OF THE TRANCE STATE, UNDERSTAND: THIS BE A MATTER OF ENTIRE FREE CHOICE OF THE ENTITY INVOLVED. HOWEVER, GROWTH HERE BE SUBLIMINAL AND THAT OF SPEED HERE THERE BE NO REQUIREMENT. IN THAT OF GROWTH PATTERN BEYOND OR OUTSIDE THAT OF THE FORMAT OF DEEP TRANCE, INDEED

HERE AN ENTITY MAY GROW AT ITS OWN RATE OF SPEED, AS FAST, SLOWER THAN, OR FASTER THAN THE ENTITY PERFORMING DEEP TRANCE.

DIR: What is the difference between you, The Echo, and what we know as the "Higher Self"?

ECHO: INDEED. INDEED HERE VERY LITTLE. IT BE MERELY THAT, AS PREVIOUS STATED, OF THE FORM ALLOWING CONTACT, THE OPENNESS OF THE HIGHER SELF TO ATTAIN THOSE INFORMATIONS THAT MAY BE PRESENTED, ASSISTED FROM THAT OF THE SPIRITUAL REALM.

DIR: Does the Higher Self consist of entities?

ECHO: INDEED. SOMEWHAT. THIS BE ENTIRE DIFFERENT MATTER HERE.

DIR: Would you call yourself a collection of Higher Selves?

ECHO: INDEED NOT. WE BE THAT, REFER IN YOUR UNDERSTANDING, ONE STEP BEYOND THAT OF HIGHER SELF.

DIR: Is Clifford's Higher Self a part of The Echo, or is it Cliff's part?

ECHO: INDEED. THAT OF REACHING INTO THE ECHO RATHER THAN A PART OF. AS IN ANY PHYSICAL ENTITY IN PERFORMANCE OF THE TRANCE STATE, THAT OF THE HIGH SELF RELEASEMENT BE REACHING INTO THAT REFER "THE CRYSTALS",
OR "COSMIC CONSCIOUSNESS", OR "THE AKASHIC RECORDS' OR WE, THE ECHO, ET CETERA.

DIR: In other words, you are the personified aspect of all those terms?

ECHO: INDEED. IN A MANNER OF SPEAKING.

DIR: Some mediums in classic English spiritualism exude ectoplasm, do various things, including forming ectoplasmic voice boxes which entities seemingly speak through. Could you please comment on the phenomenon?

ECHO: INDEED. IT INDEED BE A PHENOMENON AND BE HERE DEALING WITH THAT REFER "NECROMANCY". THIS BE NEITHER NEGATIVE OR POSITIVE, MERELY IS. IT BE A PHENOMENON THAT CERTAIN INDIVIDUALS FIND GRATIFYING AND DOES INDEED ASSIST IN THEIR GROWTH PATTERNS. HOWEVER, WE FIND THIS UNNECESSARY OF THE FORM CLIFFORD.

DIR: I have read some of the books that have come out on this, and I found them quite good, as far as understanding that there is life after death and that type of thing.

ECHO: INDEED SO. UNDERSTAND: THERE BE HERE THAT OF THE PERFORMANCE OF A SERVICE TO THOSE IN THE PHYSICAL REALM, THOSE THAT DENOUNCE SUCH ACTIVITIES, UNDERSTAND ONCE MORE, DENOUNCE MERELY THROUGH IGNORANCE ------ LACK OF UNDERSTANDING.

DIR: Sometimes Deep Trance Psychics have been referred to as "Oracles". is there any connection between that and the Seven Oracles of Delphi?

ECHO: UNDERSTAND HERE: AS THAT OF THE "SEVEN ORACLES OF DELPHI" BE IN RELATION OF COLOURS SEVEN, THAT BE PRESENTED HERE THAT OF A PRIESTHOOD THROUGH THAT OF EXTRATERRESTRIAL CONTACT.

THAT OF THE COLOURS HERE: THESE BE REFER IN THAT OF THE PHYSICAL PLANE, PLATES OF COLOUR EACH PLATE OF A SEPARATE, DIFFERENT COLOUR. HOWEVER, THESE BE SET IN A CIRCULAR PATTERN, EACH PLATE FACING EACH PLATE.

THIS THEN BE A MEANS OF COMMUNICATION AND THIS BE THAT TERMED CONSULTATION OF THE ORACLE OF DELPHI.

DIR: This would be something like some of our divining type methods, such as a chain and things like that? Is it in that category?

ECHO: INDEED NOT. RATHER HERE BE THAT OF THE SETTING OF THE COLOUR PATTERNS TO FOCUS CENTRAL POINT, IN ORDER THAT TRANSMISSION BE RECEIVED MENTALLY FROM THAT OF EXTERNAL SOURCE, HERE BE REFER "EXTRATERRESTRIAL".

DIR: OK. Now I understand.

ECHO: THE FORM OF THE ONE CLIFFORD BECOME SOMEWHAT OF RIGIDITY.

DIR: How much longer then would you suggest this session last?

ECHO: INDEED. THERE BE HERE ALLOWANCES THAT OF APPROXIMATELY FOUR MINUTES IN YOUR

TIME UNDERSTANDING. WE MUST THEN RELEASE THE FORM.

DIR: Why is it that occasionally individual personalities will speak through a Deep Trance Psychic?

ECHO: INDEED. THIS BE DUE TO THE UNDERSTANDING AND THE RESONANT REQUIREMENT OF THE ENTITY HERE PERFORMING. IT BE THAT AN ENTITY IN ITS UNDERSTANDING THAT IT BE DEALING WITH HERE "A GHOSTLY CHARACTER" OR ONE OF SPIRITUAL NATURE, IT THEN PRESENT, THROUGH ITS BEING, THAT OF THE CONTACT OF ONE.

DIR: We know that you can hear through Cliff and speak through Cliff. Do you also have the sense of smell by having access to him?

ECHO: WE MAINTAIN THAT OF THE PHYSICALNESS OF THE ENTITY.

DIR: Then is the "No Smoking " in the room a personal preference of yourself? Because there are Deep Trance Psychics where smoking is allowed.

ECHO: INDEED. AS THAT OF THE INHALING OF THE WASTE PRODUCTS OF FIRE, SUCH AS THE ONE CLIFFORD, AND WE THEN EXPERIENCE DIFFICULTY IN THE MANIPULATION OF THE VOICE BOX AND OF THE THROAT AREAS.

DIR: It has also been said that people can't touch Cliff, when he is in Trance. Why is this?

ECHO: INDEED. AS THERE BE HERE THAT OF THE ELECTROSTATIC, ELECTROMAGNETIC FORCES

108

DRAWN UPON TO ASSIST HERE. THE FORM, IN EFFECT, BE THAT WHICH BE REFER "LIGHTNING ROD". HERE, IN THAT OF THE TOUCHING, THERE BE AN INSTANT REVERSAL OF THE POLARITIES AND THE ENTITY THEN ENCOUNTER THAT OF BURNING SENSATIONS AT THE POINT OF PHYSICAL CONTACT.

DIR: Yet there have been times, when you have instructed me to rearrange his body.

ECHO: INDEED. THEN THE FIELD BE NEGATED BY WE.

DIR: Would it be possible, while Cliff is in the Deep Trance State, then to give direct healing to people, if they touched Cliff while he is in Trance? Would they be able to get healings that way?

ECHO: INDEED. WE WOULD WELCOME THE OPPORTUNITY OF ASSISTING.

DIR: Would there be the effect, like sometimes with…

ECHO: INDEED OF OCCASION AN ENTITY WILL EXPERIENCE A SUDDEN FLOW OF THE ENERGIES AND WILL LOSE CONSCIOUSNESS. THIS BE NOT THE RULE OF THUMB, HOWEVER.

DIR: Will you of The Echo, or any of you reincarnate again?

ECHO: INDEED SO. WE BE OF CONSTANT FLUCTUATION.

DIR: Is there anything you would like to say, pertaining to the discussion that we have already had, before we close?

ECHO: INDEED. THERE BE LITTLE THAT NEED BE SPOKEN HERE. MERELY THE UNDERSTANDING,

THAT THE AVAILABILITY OF ASSISTANCE BE OPEN TO ALL AND THOSE IN PERFORMANCE OF THE TRANCE STATE BE NOT DIFFERENT OR SPECIAL, MERELY THIS BE A FORMAT FOR THESE ENTITIES TO ATTAIN THOSE ASSISTANCES AND PERFORM A SERVICE TO THEIR GROWTH PATTERNS.

DIR: Thank you for this session Echo.

ECHO: WE OF THE ECHO THANK YOU OF THE OPPORTUNITY OF APPROACH.
THEREFORE HERE, WE SAY TO YOU: GO IN PEACE,
GO   IN   LOVE,   AND UNDERSTANDING.
WE RELEASE THE FORM .

Chapter 7   Psychism for beginners
1983

DIR: Indicate when the mind is clear.

ECHO: INDEED SO

DIR: Please locate and assimilate with the form of your director.

ECHO: INDEED, FORM FOUND, ASSIMILATION COMPLETE.

DIR: Is all well with the form Clifford?

ECHO: INDEED THAT OF THE FORM OF THE ONE CLIFFORD, TRANCE STATE E, LEVEL 927, BROADENING NATURALLY.

DIR: Thank you. May we proceed with questions?

ECHO: INDEED, WE WILL ASSIST TO THE UTMOST OF OUR ABILITY.

DIR: Thank You.
Echo, we were wondering if you would please give us a discourse on psychism for beginners?

ECHO: INDEED. UNDERSTAND HERE: FIRSTLY, THAT OF THE UNDERSTANDING OF THAT REFER "PSYCHISM". THIS BE MERELY THAT OF THE USE OF THE MIND. PERHAPS HERE MORE FULLY

USING THE MIND THAN TO THIS POINT IN TIME. THERE BE THAT PSYCHISM BE AN ORDINARY OCCURRENCE AND INDEED NOT THAT OF REFERENCE, "SUPERNATURAL" OR "SUPERNORMAL".

HOWEVER, THESE ENTITY BE OF HIGH DEGREE PSYCHIC ABILITY, DUE TO THAT OF THE UNFETTERING OF THE MIND IN THAT OF THE SOCIAL UNDER-- STANDINGS.

DIR: Echo, what is telepathy, and how does telepathy work between persons?

ECHO: INDEED: UNDERSTAND, THAT OF THE ENTIRE UNIVERSE BE CONSISTING OF ELECTROMAGNETISM AND ELECTROSTATISISM. IN THAT OF THE PRESENTATION OF THOUGHT FORM IN THE BRAIN OF ONE INDIVIDUAL, THERE BE AN EMANATION HERE OF MINUTE ELECTRICAL FORCE, THAT IN EFFECT COMMIT THAT THOUGHT TO THE ATMOSPHERE, AS IT WERE. ANOTHER ENTITY THEN, IN THE TUNING OF THE MIND TO THE FREQUENCY THAT BE SYNERGISTIC OF THAT ENTITY PRESENTING THOUGHT, MAY THEN RECEIVE THAT THOUGHT. UNDERSTAND: BE SIMILAR INDEED AS THAT REFER RADIO OR TELEVISION TRANSMISSIONS.

DIR: How may one increase telepathic ability?

ECHO: INDEED. IN THAT OF INCREASEMENT HERE REQUIREMENT BE ONLY AS THAT OF THE

LISTENING TO ONE'S MIND. UNDERSTAND:
MOST PHYSICAL ENTITIES BE LESS THAN
TOTALLY AWARE.

DIR: Echo, you keep referring to the mind. How do
you define and explain the mind for us?

ECHO: INDEED. HERE BE THAT OF REFERENCE
"MIND" IN ORDER THAT YOU
UNDERSTAND THAT TO WHICH WE
REFER. UNDERSTAND HERE: THERE BE
THAT OF THE MECHANICAL ACTIVITIES
WITHIN THAT REFER BRAIN.
THIS BE THAT OF ELECTRICAL SURGES,
IMPULSES, INTERLOCKS, ET CETERA. THAT
OF THE PRODUCT OF THIS ACTIVIY HERE
BE REFER "MIND" OR
INDEED "THOUGHT PATTERNS".

DIR: Echo, scientists have said that we use anywhere
from 2% to 10% of our mind or brain. Is there any
way we can use more of that, and would that
increase our potential? Would that also increase
our psychism?

ECHO: INDEED SO. UNDERSTAND: THAT OF THE
REFERENCE HERE "BRAIN" BE INDEED
GREATLY VACANT IN THAT OF THE
ANIMAL MAN. IT BE HERE THAT OF THE
INPUT, SUCH AS READINGS, STUDIES, ET
CETERA, INCREASE THAT OF THE USABLE,
RECALLING AREAS OF THE BRAIN. IT BE
MERELY A MATTER OF PERSONAL
BUILDING, DEVELOPMENT OF THE BRAIN.

DIR: And stirring the imagination?

ECHO: INDEED SO.

DIR: A lot of people look down on the imagination as not based in fact.

ECHO: UNDERSTAND HERE; THROUGHOUT THAT REFER "AGES", IN YOUR UNDER-STANDING, THOSE ENTITIES THAT BE IN USE OF COMPARITIVELY MORE OF BRAIN, BE OBSERVED BY THOSE ENTITY IN POWER AS BEING THREATENING, DANGEROUS ENTITY, AS ENTITY THAT THINK FOR ITS OWN BEING INDEED THEN DO NOT FOLLOW THE DICTATES OF ANOTHER.
THIS THEN BE OBSERVED AS DANGEROUS IN THE EYES OF THOSE IN CONTROL. THROUGHOUT YOUR RECORDED HISTORY THIS BE REPEATED TIME AND TIME AND TIME AGAIN, WHEN THOSE REFER "THINKERS", DEVELOPERS BE PROSECUTED AND INCARCERATED. THEREFORE, A PRESENTATION TO THAT OF THE MASSES THAT OF THE IMAGINATION BE ABSTRACT OCCURRENCE WORTHY OF LITTLE ATTENTION. THIS THEN LEAD THAT OF THE MASSES TO BELIEVE IT TO BE SUCH AS "ONLY MY IMAGINATION".

DIR: Echo, are we born with fully developed psychic talents, or is psychic ability something a person needs to develop?

ECHO: INDEED. UNDERSTAND HERE: EACH AND EVERY ENTITY BORN IN A STATE OF HEALTH BE IN TOTAL CONTROL OF ITS PSYCHIC ABILITIES. IT BE AS THAT IN

114

THAT OF THE NEGATIVE PROGRAMMING OF EARLY CHILDHOOD, THIS PSYCHIC ABILITY BE THEN FORCED WITHIN AND IN EFFECT SQUELCHED IN A MAJOR PORTION OF THE POPULATION.

DIR: Is this the reason why strong people seem to have more natural psychic talent? Is it that they are free of programming?

ECHO: INDEED. OF SOMEWHAT HERE.

DIR: Are there other reasons?

ECHO: INDEED. THERE ARE SOME ENTITIES, THAT THERE BE THOSE THAT WILL NOT BE SUBDUED, AND THESE MAINTAIN THROUGH THE GROWING OF THE ENTITY THAT OF THE INHERENT PSYCHIC ABILITIES. OTHER ENTITY, UPON THE DESIRE OF LEARNING MORE, APPROACH OTHERS AND UNDERGO TRAININGS THAT WILL ALLOW THE VIEWING OF THEMSELVES WITHOUT THAT OF REFERENCE HERE, "NEGATIVE PROGRAMMINGS".

DIR: Echo, one of the most common things that people say are: "I have a feeling of being there before", or "this has happened to me before", or "I have had the same conversation before". Would you explain that, please?

ECHO: INDEED SO. THIS THERE BE REFER TO THAT OF "DEJA VUE".

HERE UNDERSTAND: IN MOST INSTANCES HERE IT BE THAT THE ENTITY HAVE

115

INDEED PREVIOUS ENCOUNTERED THE OCCURRENCE OR LOCATION THAT IT BE VIEWING. IN THIS MANNER THE ENTITY IN THE FORM OF THAT REFER "ASTRAL TRAVEL" HAS BROKEN THAT REFER "TIME BARRIERS" AND IN THE SLEEP STATE HAVE ASTRALLED AND ENCOUNTERED THAT WHICH IT BE VIEWING IN THE PHYSICAL.

DIR: What exactly then is Astralling?

ECHO: INDEED. THIS BE THAT OF THE REMOVAL, THE FREEDOM OF THE MIND, AS THAT REFER "ASTRAL BODY" HERE, RELEASING FROM THAT OF THE PHYSICAL BODY AND TRAVELING IN THAT OF THE SPIRITUAL REALM.
UNDERSTAND HERE: EACH ENTITY EXISTING IN THE PHYSICAL BE BOTH PHYSICAL AND SPIRITUAL AT ONCE AND THE SAME TIME. MOST ENTITIES IN THAT STATE REFER "SLEEP" DO INDEED ASTRAL.

DIR: You say "most". Are there some people who don't?

ECHO: INDEED. THERE BE SOME ENTITIES, DUE TO RESTRICTIVENESS OF CHARACTER THAT INDEED WILL NOT ALLOW THAT OF REFERENCE HERE "THE SEPARATION OF THE ASTRAL BODY".

DIR: So attitudes play a great portion in psychic development?

ECHO: INDEED SO. UNDERSTAND: THOSE DEALING IN NEGATIVITY WILL ENCOUNTER DIFFICULTY IN GROWTH PATTERNS IN RELATION THAT OF DEVELOPMENT OF PSYCHIC ABILITIES. POSITIVITY HERE BE THE ANSWER. LOVE OF THE FELLOW MAN, APPROACH THAT OF THE PSYCHISM WITH LOVE AND DEDICATION OF PURPOSE AND THERE BE FINE RESULTS FOR ANY AND ALL ENTITIES.

DIR: Why are there so many people today, who have a fear of psychism?

ECHO: INDEED. UNDERSTAND; THAT OF THE FEAR OF PSYCHISM THERE BE BASED FIRSTLY IN THAT OF RELIGION, THAT HERE IT BE PREACHED THAT PSYCHISM BE "WORKS OF EVIL". UNDERSTAND HERE: IT BE A MANNER OF CONTROL OF THE POPULACE. ALSO HERE QUERY WE OFFER TO THEE FOR FOOD FOR THOUGHT: WHY INDEED WOULD AN ENTITY FIND FEAR IN OCCURRENCE WITHIN THE MIND OF SELF? BE THIS NOT PART AND PARCEL OF THE WHOLE ENTITY?

DIR: Echo, often , we have people come to us, who say they are afraid of the psychic, because the only thing they seem to know in advance are terrible things?

ECHO: INDEED. REFERENCE HERE: "TERRIBLE THINGS"'?

DIR: Well, they sometimes see an accident or somebody dying and think that's the only area that they have of psychic abilities.

ECHO: INDEED SO. UNDERSTAND: THAT OF THE VIEWING OF AN ENTITY IN CROSSING BE INDEED NOT A "TERRIBLE THING", AS THAT OF THE TERM "TERRIBLE THING" HERE BE A SOCIAL CONNOTATION. UNDERSTAND: ALL.. ENTITIES IN THE PHYSICAL REALM WILL INDEED ATTAIN "CROSSING" TO THAT OF THE SPIRITUAL REALM. IN THE VIEWING OF THE ACCIDENT, ET CETERA, IT INDEED BE A PSYCHIC OCCURRENCE. HOWEVER, THE ENTITY VIEWING HERE NEED NOT MAKE SOCIAL JUDGEMENT THAT THIS BE A TERRIBLE THING NOR THE JUDGMENT THAT THE VIEWER HAVE A RESPONS-IBILITY OF THE CHANGING OF THIS OCCURRENCE.

UNDERSTAND; WHEN ONE WATCHES A MOVING PICTURE ONE DOES NOT ATTEMPT TO STOP THE VILLIAN FROM SHOOTING THE HERO. ONE LEAVES THE VIEWING SAYING TO THEMSELVES: "THIS WAS AN INTERESTING MOVING PICTURE" OR "THIS WAS A GOOD PICTURE". UNDERSTAND: THAT OF THE PSYCHIC VIEWING BE INDEED SIMILAR FORMAT, AS THAT OF THE VIEWING BE JUST THAT: THE VIEWING. THERE BE HERE NO RESPONSIBILITY ATTACHED.

DIR: Do they have a responsibility to tell the person?

ECHO: INDEED NOT. UNDERSTAND: AS THAT OF THE LIFE EXPERIENCE OF EACH ENTITY IN THE PHYSICAL REALM BE SINGULAR AND SEPARATE TO EACH ENTITY. THAT OF THE OCCURRENCE OF THAT STATED "ACCIDENT", HERE MAY INDEED BE PART OF THE LIFE EXPERIENCE OF THAT ENTITY.
THE ENTITY VIEWING HAVE NEITHER THE RESPONSIBILITY NOR RIGHT OF THE MAKING OF THAT JUDGMENT FOR ANOTHER.

DIR: Why is it that they feel that all they have is the frightening side?

ECHO: INDEED. IT BE BASED IN THAT OF THE PROGRAMMING OF THE ENTITY, AS PREVIOUSLY STATED. ALSO THERE BE THAT OF THE CONNOTATION ATTACHED TO PSYCHIC PHENOMENON, THAT BE PRESENTED AS WEIRD, AS EVIL, AND THEREFORE IN THE MINDS OF THESE ENTITIES ONLY THEIR VIEWED EVIL WILL APPEAR.

DIR: Echo, could you tell us the importance of dreams in a person's awareness of their psychic abilities?

ECHO: INDEED SO. UNDERSTAND: THAT OF THE FORMAT "DREAM" HERE BE OF SEVERAL FORMATS. PRIMARILY IT BE THAT OF A DISCUSSION BETWEEN THAT REFER "SUBCONSCIOUSNESS" OF THE ENTITY AND THE CONSCIOUSNESS OF THE ENTITY. IT BE THAT OF THE SUBCONSCIOUSNESS PRESENT

119

INFORMATION IN THE SYMBOLOGY OF THE ENTITY DREAMING.

THEREFORE UNDERSTAND: WHEN ONE REQUESTS ANOTHER TO ANALYZE IT'S DREAM, THAT OTHER, ATTEMPTING TO ANALYZE, HAVE SEVERE DIFFICULTY, AS THE SYMBOLOGY PRESENTED BE SINGULAR TO THAT OF THE ENTITY DREAMING. THEREFORE HERE: EACH AND EVERY ENTITY ANALYZE ITS DREAMS, ANALYZE ITS SYMBOLOGY AND THE MESSAGE OF THE SUBCONSCIOUS BE THEN REALIZED.

ALSO HERE, THAT WHICH OFT-TIMES BE VIEWED DREAMING RATHER BE THAT OF REMEMBERANCE OF THE ASTRAL EXPERIENCE AND HERE THE ENTITY MAY GAIN INSIGHTS INTO SELF AND OTHERS THROUGH THAT OF THE UNDERSTANDING OF THE ASTRAL EXPERIENCE.

DIR: I have talked to a number of people, who have told me that one of the reasons why they don't remember their dreams at night is because they have nightmares a lot of the time. Why does this happen?

ECHO: INDEED. UNDERSTAND: AS PREVIOUS SPOKEN, THAT OF THE DREAM BE A MESSAGE OF THE SUBCONSCIOUS TO THE CONSCIOUS OF THE ENTITY. NIGHTMARES ALSO BE THE SAME FORMAT. THE ENTITY HERE, IN THAT OF THE REMEMBERANCE OF THE NIGHTMARES, IN ALL LIKELIHOOD HERE WILL DISCOVER MESSAGES BEING PRESENTED TO THE CONSCIOUSNESS OF THE ENTITY THAT

WILL BE OPPOSITION TO SOMETHING OCCURRING WITHIN THE CONSCIOUS LIFE OF THE ENTITY.

DIR: So it's not necessarily a negative thing. Then people shouldn't really be fearful about it.

ECHO: INDEED. NOTHING NEGATIVE WHATSOEVER. IT BE HERE PROVEN TIME AND AGAIN: EVEN THOSE NIGHTMARES THAT APPEAR VIOLENT OR NEGATIVE, PRESENT POSITIVITY TO THE CONSCIOUSNESS OF THE ENTITY. EXAMPLE HERE BE OF ENTITY DREAMING OF BEING FLOODED IN BLOOD. THE ENTITY OBSERVE THIS HIGHLY NEGATIVELY AND FRIGHTENINGLY. UPON CLOSER EXAMINATION IT BE FOUND THE ENTITY IN CONSCIOUS STATE BE A KILLER OF ANIMALS, BE THAT REFER SLAUGHTERHOUSE BUTCHER AND THE ENTITY IN REALITY DEEP INSIDE THE MIND BE IN TOTAL REVULSION OF THE KILLING ACT. UPON THE LEARNING OF THIS FACT, THE ENTITY DISCOVER NO FURTHER NIGHTMARES AND FIND A CHANGE IN THE FORMAT OF HIS CONSCIOUS EXISTENCE.

DIR: Echo: Freud said that the subconscious is something that must be suppressed, the conscious mind must be in absolute control. Would you care to comment on that, when psychism is supposed to come from the subconscious?

ECHO: INDEED: UNDERSTAND: THAT OF REFERENCE "SIGMUND FREUD" BE

INDEED LEARNED GENTLEMAN. HOWEVER, THE ENTITY TAUGHT THAT OF THE UNKNOWN FROM AN OBSERVATION OF HIGH DEGREE OF RIGIDITY. THIS ENTITY, IN ITS EXPERIMENTATION, IN ITS STUDIES, MOVE ON THE ASSUMPTION THAT ALL OCCURRENCES WITHIN THE MIND MAY BE TRACED TO OCCURRENCES WITHIN THIS PHYSICAL REINCARNATION. UNDERSTAND HERE WE SAY TO YOU THIS BE UNTRUE.

DIR: Before we go into more of that, I have to turn the tape over. Echo, at this time, can you tell me what level the form of Clifford is at. Please?

ECHO: INDEED. THE FORM OF THE ONE CLIFFORD: TRANCE STATE J, LEVEL 9524, MAINTAINING.

DIR: Thank you.

OK. So you mentioned reincarnation as part of psychism. Could you please expand on that more?

ECHO: INDEED. HERE SOMEWHAT CORRECTION OF THIS STATEMENT; REINCARNATION BE INDEED INHERENT PART OF THE PHYSICAL ENTITY MAN AND THAT OF' PSYCHISM BE INHERENT PART OF THE PHYSICAL ENTITY MAN.

DIR: Is there any difference between Psychism and Spirituality

ECHO: INDEED. VERY LITTLE. MERELY HERE A MATTER OF SEMANTICS.

DIR: ECHO: For a long time I felt that Spirituality had to do with Religion?

ECHO: INDEED SO. UNDERSTAND: THAT OF REFERENCE "RELIGION", INDEED THAT OF THE POWER OF PRAYER BE REAL, BE SOLID, IT BE THAT OF THE CASTING OF THOUGHT TO THE ATMOSPHERE. THAT OF THE THOUGHT BE A WHOLE, A SOLID ENTITY UNTO ITSELF.

HOWEVER, THAT REFER "RELIGIONS" HAVE HERE AS STANDARD FORMAT THAT OF THE FOLLOWING OF ANOTHER AND THAT OF THE CONTROL OF THE POPULACE IN ORDER THAT THE RELIGION MAY GROW AND FLOURISH.
UNDERSTAND: THAT OF THE FORM OF JESUS OF NAZARETH HAVE PRESENT TO THE WORLD THAT EACH AND EVERY ENTITY MAY DO AS HE AND YET BETTER, AND YET IN MAN'S IGNORANCE OF THE USE OF THE NATURAL FORCES, MAN HAS BECOME A FOLLOWER[1] RATHER THAN THAT OF A SELF-LEADER.

DIR: OK. You mention prayer as being a very real thing. Then there is the term "meditation". Some people tend to couple them together. Perhaps you can define the two terms: Prayer and Meditation for us.

123

ECHO: INDEED. IN THAT OF THE USUAL FORMAT PRAYER, IT BE THAT OF THE REQUESTING OF ASSISTANCE FROM AN EXTERIOR FORCE.

THAT OF THE MEDITATION BE THAT OF THE DEMANDING ASSISTANCE THROUGH THE USE OF AN INTERIOR FORCE AND THEN CONTROLLING, SOMEWHAT, THAT OF THE NATURAL EXTERIOR FORCES.

DIR: Does meditation go hand in hand with psychism?

ECHO: INDEED SO, AS DOES PRAYER. HOWEVER, THAT OF THE RELIGIOUS FORMAT PRAYER BE OF RESTRICTIVE NATURE, RATHER THAN EXPANSIVE NATURE. THAT OF THE FORMAT MEDITATION ASSIST IN THE OPENING OF THE MIND, THE DEVELOPING OF THE MIND AND INDEED THAT OF THE BUILDING OF THAT REFER PSYCHISM.

DIR: Echo: I'd like to talk about some of the things, that people in developing psychism might find a bit frightening, or things that have happened to them, that made them aware that something else was going on.

Myself, just as I lay down to relax, this was not meditation, this was just something that happened, I used to experience a weight on my back and I found this very, very frightening and it was years before I found out what it was. Perhaps you could explain this to other people, who, I am sure, have experienced the same type of thing?

ECHO: INDEED. FIRSTLY HERE: THAT OF THE GREAT WEIGHT UPON BEING BE OF TWOFOLD HERE IN THAT OF THE GRADUAL OPENING, DEVELOPMENT OF THE MIND,

THE ENTITY RECEIVE THAT TERMED "A NUDGE". HERE THIS BE THAT
OF THE ENCOUNTER OF THE SPIRITUAL ENERGIES THAT BE PERCIEVED BY THE ENTITY AS THE WEIGHT UPON THE BEING. BE REFER OCCASIONALLY AS THAT OF THE "GUIDE", THE "SPIRITUAL GUIDE", RESTING UPON THE CHEST, IN ORDER THAT THE ENTITY MAY BE MADE FURTHER AWARE. ALSO HERE IT BE THAT OF THE MIND OF THE ENTITY BEING MADE, CORRECTION, OPENING TO THE POINT OF AWARENESS OF THE NATURAL. CONSTRUCTION OF THE UNIVERSE AS THAT OF MOLECULAR ELECTRICAL STRUCTURE OF THE EARTH AND THIS BE PERCEIVED OCCASIONALLY AS THE WEIGHTLESSNESS OF THE BODY OR WEIGHTFULNESS OF THE BODY.

DIR: There was also another happening that used to just absolutely terrify me, and that was my bed used to shake at night.
1 convinced myself that it was traffic, anything, but nevertheless it frightened me. I would sleep with my light on.

ECHO: INDEED. THE ENTITY THERE BE IN SUDDEN AWARENESS OF ALL THE SO-CALLED HORROR MOVIES IT HAS EVER VIEWED UNDERSTAND: THAT OF REFERENCE "HORROR MOVIE" ALSO HERE BE IN A MANNER OF THE PRESENTATION OF THE NEGATIVE UNDERSTANDING TO THAT OF THE MASSES. THIS BE ALSO MANNER OF CONTROL, SOMEWHAT, OF MASSES, AS THE INSTALLATION OF FEAR BE A FINE

FORMAT OF CONTROLLING MASSES, THAT THOSE IN THE MASSES WILL NOT THEN LOOK FURTHER WITHIN OR WITHOUT OF SELVES.
IN THAT OF THE FORMAT HERE OF THE SHAKING OF THE BED, IT BE THAT, AT THE POINT OF DEVELOPMENT OF SPIRITUAL ASPECTS OF THIS ENTITY, THERE BE HERE A MELDING WITH THAT OF THE UNIVERSE, A DEVELOPMENT OF THE SUBCONSCIOUS KNOWLEDGE OF THE USE OF THE NATURAL ENERGIES, NATURAL FORCES AND THESE THROUGH THE SUBCONSCIOUSNESS BE MADE EVIDENT TO THE CONSCIOUSNESS OF THE ENTITY.

DIR: Echo: I have had some experiences, that I had when 1 was a child, that I found quite frightening.
When 1 was around 11 or 12 years old, just at the age of puberty, before I fell asleep at night, I used to see these terrifying frightening faces on the wall, just as I was falling asleep.
I also used to get a sensation that I was sleeping in quicksand, as I was falling off, and this caused me at that age to be quite fearful going to sleep.
What would be some of the reasons for this?

ECHO: INDEED. THIS BE RESULTINGS OF THE PROGRAMMING THAT THE ENTITY HAVE ENCOUNTERED PREVIOUS TO THE EVENTS. THIS ENTITY EXIST IN CHILDHOOD IN THAT OF HIGH DEGREE OF RESTRICTIVE RULES AND REGULATIONS IN ITS SURROUNDINGS. THE ENTITY HAVE PRESENTED TO IT, OF MANY TIMES, THAT IF IT DO NOT SUCH AND SUCH, THEN

CERTAIN NEGATIVE HAPPENINGS WILL. OCCUR, SUCH AS THE BOGEYMAN, SUCH AS "GOD WILL GET YOU", SUCH AS "YOU ARE A CHILD OF THE DEVIL", ET CETERA, ET CETERA.
WHAT ELSE MAY ONE EXPECT, WHEN NEGATIVE PROGRAMMING BE PRESENTED TO THE SUBCONSCIOUSNESS OF AN ENTITY?

DIR: How can parents help their children grow up without fear of their psychic abilities?

ECHO: INDEED. DEVELOP THE CHILD THROUGH LOVE, RATHER THAN FEAR. IT BE THAT SIMPLE.

DIR: Echo: Some people are, again, afraid of ghosts. Can you perhaps, say what they are, and go on about that, please?

ECHO: INDEED. THAT OF REFERENCE "GHOST" BE THAT OF A MANIFESTATION OF ONE RESIDING 1N THE SPIRITUAL REALM, MANIFESTING IN THE PHYSICAL TO THE POINT OF VIEWING BY THOSE IN THE PHYSICAL REALM. AS THIS BE, HERE IN - ONCE MORE-- GENERAL TERMS, IN MOST INSTANCES THIS BE THAT OF
AN ENTITY THAT BE SOMEWHAT EARTHBOUND EMOTIONALLY, MENTALLY, DUE TO OCCURRENCES PRIOR TO CROSSING OR THAT OF THE NEEDS OF PASSING OF INFORMATION TO THOSE IN THE PHYSICAL REALM

IN THE VIEWING OF A GHOST, UNDERSTAND, IT BE JUST THAT: VIEWING. THERE BE NO HARMFUL EFFECT, UNLESS AN ENTITY ALLOW FEAR HERE TO OVERTAKE ITS BEING. THIS BE THE ONLY FORMAT, THAT MAY CREATE DIFFICULTY FOR THOSE IN THE PHYSICAL REALM.

DIR: What about Poltergeist phenomena?

ECHO: INDEED. UNDERSTAND HERE: THAT OF POLTERGEIST PHENOMENON BE THAT OF THE FRUSTRATED ENTITY EITHER IN THE PHYSICAL OR SPIRITUAL REALM. POLTERGEIST ACTIVITY MAY BE ATTRIBUTED TO THAT OF THE PSYCHOKINETIC ACTIVITY AND/OR THAT OF FRUSTRATED SPIRITUAL ACTIVITY.

IN THE DESIRE OF REMOVAL OF THIS IT REQUIRE MERELY CONFRONTATION OF SPIRITUAL ENTITY AND THE SENDING OF THE ENTITY ON ITS WAY.

DIR: What if it is a frustrated physical entity?

ECHO: INDEED. THIS THEN REQUIRE EITHER THE BUILDING OF THIS TALENT, THE UNDERSTANDING OF THIS TALENT, OR THE REMOVAL OF THIS TALENT, THAT WHICH THE ENTITY DESIRE.

DIR: Thanks. A lot of people, who start thinking about psychic phenomena start running into things like: psychics don't believe in God and are dealing into witchcraft and black magic and all those terms. Could you please enlighten us on that?

ECHO: INDEED. FIRST OF ALL, HERE, WE OF THE ECHO "POO-PAH" THIS STATEMENT UNDERSTAND: THOSE DEALING IN THAT REFER "PSYCHISM" DEAL WITH THAT REFER "POSITIVITY AND LOVE OF FELLOW MAN". THOSE DEALING IN NEGATIVITY, DEAL IN HATRED, DEAL IN AFFLICTION OF THE FELLOW MAN.

THIS BE SEPARATE AND APART AND HERE DO UNDERSTAND: THERE BE THE NATURAL LAW OF EXISTENCE. IT BE "LIKE ATTRACT LIKE" AND THIS IN THIS UNDERSTANDING HERE BE:

WHEN ONE DEAL IN NEGATIVITY, ONE RECEIVE NEGATIVITY IN RETURN. WHEN ONE DEAL IN POSITIVITY, ONE FIND POSITIVITY IN RETURN.

THOSE DEALING IN THE DEVELOPMENT OF THE MIND, ERGO PSYCHIC, IN THE VAST MAJORITY HAVE STRONG FAITH IN THAT REFER "GOD" AND MAINTAIN LITTLE OR NO BELIEF IN THAT REFER "DEVIL" OR "EVIL".

THOSE PRESENTING FROM THAT OF THE RELIGIOUS STANDING, THE BELIEF THAT PSYCHICS DEAL IN EVIL, UNDERSTAND: THESE ENTITIES THEN BE DEALING IN NEGATIVITY TOWARD FELLOW MAN. THIS THEN, WE OFFER TO YOU, BE EVIL.

DIR: So, then the terms of witchcraft and magic are not necessarily negative?

ECHO: INDEED NOT. UNDERSTAND: THAT REFER "WITCHCRAFT" BE ALSO THAT REFER "WICCA", ALSO THAT REFER "OLD RELIGION", FAR, FAR PRIOR THAT REFER "CHRISTIANITY". UNDERSTAND: THAT OF THE OLD TESTAMENT OF THE BIBLE DEAL WITH THAT OF THE OLD RELIGION OR THAT REFER "WICCA, WITCHCRAFT". UNDERSTAND: IT BE THAT OF REFERENCE HERE "CHRISTIANITY" THAT DO LABEL WITCHCRAFT NEGATIVE. UNDERSTAND HERE, HOWEVER, THERE BE SOME INDIVIDUALS, THAT DEAL IN WICCA IN NEGATIVE ASPECTS. THESE ENTITIES BE BEST AVOIDED.

DIR: Thank you, Echo. Is there any thing you would like to say before we close?
I've got one more question: Could you give us a perceptive exercise or technique, that a beginner could use to unlock their psychic abilities?

ECHO: INDEED. FIRSTLY, THAT OF A MEDITATIVE PROCESS HERE, THAT OF ATTAINING SPACE AND TIME WITHOUT INTERRUPTION, NOISE, ET CETERA. THE ENTITY MAKE ITS BEING PRONE AND THEN RELAX THE MUSCULAR STRUCTURES OF THE BODY AS IN THAT REFER "PROGRESSIVE RELAXATION". IT THEN ALLOW THE MIND FREEDOM TO FLOW, PAY ATTENTION TO THAT OF SMALL, TINY, SECONDARY THOUGHTS, THAT APPEAR IN SUDDEN FLASHES IN THE MIND. THE ENTITY WILL RECEIVE PICTURE IMPRESSIONS AND MAY THEN THINK ABOUT FRIENDS, RELATIVES,

AND WHAT THOSE FRIENDS AND RELATIVES ARE DOING AT THAT PRECISE SECOND THE IMPRESSION PRIMARY, THAT BE RECEIVED HERE, BE THAT IMPRESSION TO BE ACTED OR THOUGHT UPON. 1N THE PRACTICE OF THIS FORMAT AN ENTITY MAY ASSIST IN THE OPENING OF ITS MIND. ALSO, THERE BE TRAININGS, ASSISTANCES THAT BE AVAILABLE THROUGH SUCH AS THOSE PRESENT, THAT MAY ASSIST OTHERS TO LEARN MORE FULLY.

DIR: OK. Echo, Thank you very much for this session. Is there anything you'd like to say in closing?

ECHO: INDEED. FIRSTLY HERE:

FEAR NOT THE MIND OF SELF, AS SELF BE HERE IN CONTROL.

WHEN ANOTHER INFORM YOU THAT WHICH YOU ARE DOING WITH YOUR MIND BE EVIL, DO UNDERSTAND; THAT ENTITY BE IN EFFORT OF CONTROL OF YOU. BEYOND THIS, LITTLE OF PRESENT..

DIR: Thank you for this session, Echo.

ECHO: INDEED. WE OF THE ECHO THANK YOU OF THE OPPORTUNITY OF APPROACH. THEREFORE HERE, WE SAY TO YOU: GO IN PEACE, GO IN LOVE AND UNDERSTANDING.

WE RELEASE THE FORM.

Chapter 8   Meditation and Relaxation

DIR: Please clear the mind. Indicate when the mind is cleared.

ECHO: INDEED. HERE THE MIND BE CLEARED.

DIR: Please locate and assimilate with the form of your director.

ECHO: INDEED. THE ONE DIRECTOR BE FOUND.

DIR: Is all well with the form of Clifford?

ECHO: INDEED. THE FORM OF THE ONE CLIFFORD, TRANCE STATE 6. LEVEL 521--BROADENING NATURALLY.

DIR: May we proceed with questions?

ECHO: INDEED. WE WILL ASSIST TO THE UTMOST OF OUR ABILITIES.

DIR: OK. Echo, we would like to do a session on meditation and relaxation. Would you like to give us an opening statement, please?

ECHO: INDEED. UNDERSTAND HERE: THAT OF REFERENCE "MEDITATION, RELAXATION" INDEED BE ONE AND THE SAME, YET SOMEWHAT SEPARATE AND APART AN ENTITY MAY MEDITATE IN THAT OF QUIETUDE, SOLITUDE, RELAXATION AND YET IT MAY RELAX AND MEDITATE WHILE IT BE IN PERFORMANCE OF A

PHYSICAL FUNCTION. MEDITATION, THEN BE THAT FORMAT OF THE DRAWING WITHIN, THE EXPANDING OF THE CONSCIOUSNESS OF AN ENTITY AND THE GAINING FOR SELF THAT OF MENTAL, EMOTIONAL RELAXATION.

DIR: Is meditation necessary, then?

ECHO: INDEED. UNDERSTAND: THERE BE HERE NOT THAT OF NECESSITY. RATHER THAT ALL ENTITIES INDEED DO MEDITATE. HOWEVER, THERE BE DIFFERENCES HERE, MERELY IN DEGREE.

DIR: OK. You already mentioned that relaxation and meditation are very close to being synonymous. How does meditation affect the physical body and self?

ECHO: INDEED. UNDERSTAND HERE: FIRSTLY: THAT OF THE BRAIN, THE MIND, CONTROL THE PHYSICAL BODY OF AN ENTITY. THEN IT NATURALLY FOLLOW IN THE CONTROL OF THE BRAIN, MIND, THE BODY BE THEN MAINTAINED IN THAT STATE OF WHICH THE ENTITY BE DESIROUS. THEREFORE, MEDITATION BE INDEED OF A HEALING FORMAT OF REFERENCE "PHYSICAL BODY".

DIR: OK. So, how does meditation affect the etheric body, the etheric shell?

ECHO: INDEED. SOMEWHAT IN THAT OF SAME MANNER. YET IN THAT OF THE ETHERIC DEALINGS HERE, THERE BE THAT OF THE MAKING AVAILABLE TO THE

PHYSICAL ENTITY EASIER ACCESS TO THAT OF THE USE OF THE ETHERIC ENERGIES OF THE ETHERIC BODY. THIS THEN GO HAND IN HAND WITH THAT OF THE HEALING PROCESSES OF THE PHYSICAL BODY. UNDERSTAND: RATHER THAN THE TREATING OF A SYMPTOM OR EFFECT, RATHER TREAT THAT OF THE CAUSING AND OF THE ENTIRE PHYSICAL, MENTAL, EMOTIONAL, SPIRITUAL AND INDEED ETHERIC ENTITY.

DIR: I am going through all the types of bodies here. Can we deal, specifically, with the mental body? How does meditation affect the mental body?

ECHO: INDEED. NOW THERE BE HERE THROUGH THE FORMAT MEDITATION, THAT OF THE QUIETING OF THE MENTAL PROCESSES, THAT OF THE REALIZATION THAT THE MUNDANE INDEED BE MUNDANE, AND THIS THEM ASSISTS IN TURN IN THE QUIETING, IN THE PEACE OF MIND.

DIR: Then meditation reduces stress. Is it possible to reduce stress without meditation?

ECHO: INDEED NOT. UNDERSTAND: EVEN THE WOODMAN CHOPPING A TREE BE IN A FORM OF MEDITATION. AS THOSE IN REFERENCE "LAND OF JAPAN" THAT BE IN ENTRY INTO "FRUSTRATION ROOM" AND HERE INFLICT VIOLENCE UPON THAT OF FABRIC BEING, INDEED BE EXERCISING A FORM OF MEDITATION. HERE IT BE INDEED THAT OF REDUCTION OF STRESS FACTORS.

DIR: Punching a bag doesn't seem to me like meditation. That's really physical.

ECHO: INDEED NOT. UNDERSTAND: MEDITATION ORIGINATES WITHIN THE MIND OF THE INDIVIDUAL, AND THAT WHICH THE INDIVIDUAL FIND COMFORTING INDEED BE MEDITATION.

DIR: How does meditation, a person going into meditation, how does it affect the spiritual self or the spiritual nature of that individual?

ECHO: INDEED. THROUGH THAT OF UNDERSTANDING. HERE THERE BE AN ENTITY IN THAT REFER "MEDITATIVE STATE," BE INTROSPECTIVE, BE EXAMINING THAT OF THE INNER ANIMAL, AND IN THIS MANNER THERE BE UNDERSTANDINGS PRESENTED FROM THE SUBCONSCIOUSNESS OF THE ENTITY TO THE CONSCIOUSNESS OF THE ENTITY. THESE UNDERSTANDINGS THEN ASSIST IN THAT OF THE PERSONAL GROWTH PATTERNS AND THIS IN TURN, THEN, BE IN REALITY, DEVELOPMENT FURTHER, OF SPIRITUAL RESONANCE.

DIR: How does meditation affect the emotional nature?

ECHO: INDEED. AS PREVIOUSLY STATED, EMOTIONS BE MANIFESTED OF MIND AND OFT-TIMES BE HIGHLY RELATIVE TO THAT OF SOCIAL STRUCTURE OF THE ENVIRONMENT IN WHICH THE ENTITY EXISTS. IN THAT OF THE MEDITATION THE ENTITY THEN VIEW THE REALITY OF THIS SITUATION AND THE EMOTIONS BE QUIETED, RELAXED.

THIS BE MOST NOTICEABLE IN THAT FORMAT REFER "JUDGMENTALISM" AND ANGERS.

DIR: Echo, the general opinion is that one can't grow spiritually, unless one meditates. Is this true?

ECHO: THERE BE THAT "GENERAL OPINION" OF WHOM?

DIR: Well, it seems that I have heard that in discussions for a long time. I can't put it to any one particular person. It seems to be a general prerequisite to enlightenment.

ECHO: INDEED. UNDERSTAND: THERE BE INDEED THAT OF ASSISTMENT HERE. HOWEVER, AND ENTITY IN ITS CHOICES MAY FOREGO THAT FORMAT HERE REFER "STANDARD MEDITATIONS". AN ENTITY MAY INDEED MEDITATE WITHIN ITS BEING REGARDLESS OF PHYSICAL ACTIVITY.

DIR: So formal meditation is not absolutely necessary, taking so many minutes off per day, in formally meditating?

ECHO: INDEED NOT. BE A MATTER OF CHOICE OF THE ENTITY HERE. SHOULD AN ENTITY FEEL THE NEED OF ALONENESS, SEPARATENESS, QUIETUDE, INDEED SO IT AVAIL ITS BEING OF AN OPPORTUNITY TO PERFORM SO. HOWEVER, AN ENTITY IN THAT OF THE UNDERSTANDING OF THE MEDITATION MAY INDEED MEDITATE DAILY OF THAT OF THE HUNDREDS OF TIMES, THEREBY CREATE THAT OF A FLOWING MEDITATIVE STATE, AS IT WERE. IN THIS MANNER, THE ENTITY WILL DISCOVER LITTLE OF DIFFICULTY IN

RELATION THAT REFER ANGER$_1$
FRUSTRATIONS, ETC.

DIR: Echo, when a person is in that meditative state continually, like you just suggested, does that not make the person more open to suggestions?

ECHO: INDEED NOT. HERE, DO NOT ASSUME THAT MEDITATION, AS WE SPEAK, OF THE ENTERING ALTERED STATE. HERE UNDERSTAND: MEDITATION BE THAT OF THE DEALING WITH THE UNDERSTANDINGS OF OCCURRENCES ABOUT THE ENTITY. THAT OF ALTERED STATE HERE BE ENTIRE SEPARATE AND APART OF MEDITATION, AS IT WERE.

DIR: Does meditation affect males and females similarly? Is it exactly the same, or are there differences?

ECHO: INDEED. THERE BE NO DIFFERENCE HERE. UNDERSTAND: THAT THE MIND OF THE MALE AND THE MIND OF THE FEMALE BE IDENTICAL, EXCEPT IN RELATION THAT OF THE PHYSICAL BODIES. THOUGHT PROCESSES OF THE MALE AND FEMALE BE IDENTICAL, AS THERE BE THAT OF SPIRITUAL ENTITY THAT BE SEXLESS IN ORIGIN AND MERELY IN THAT OF THE INHABITING OF A PHYSICAL BODY, MUST THEN INDUCE ACCEPTANCE OF SEXUAL CONNOTATIONS.

DIR: Is it beneficial for a person to be relaxed all of the time, or is a certain amount of stress beneficial for the system?

ECHO: INDEED SO. UNDERSTAND: STRESS BE THAT WHICH MANIFESTS CIRCULATION, MANIFESTS TONING OF PHYSICAL BODY, ETC., ETC.. STRESS BE INDEED WITH THE PHYSICAL

ENTITY AT ALL TIMES. HOWEVER, THE ENTITY MAY ALSO HAVE WITH IT, AT ALL TIMES THAT OF THE FORMAT MEDITATION. UNDERSTAND HERE: STRESS BE AN INHERENT FACTOR OF THE PHYSICAL EXISTENCE.

DIR: Many people include prayer and meditation as the same thing. Are prayer and meditation the same?

ECHO: INDEED SO. IN AN MANNER OF SPEAKING. REMEMBER THAT MEDITATION BE THAT OF A PRODUCT OF THE MIND. PRAYER THEN BE A PRODUCT OF MEDITATION.

DIR: Why is it that western culture finds very much difficulty in grasping meditative concepts?

ECHO: ALAS... THAT OF THE REFERENCE HERE "WESTERN CULTURE", THESE HAVE ASSUMED THEIR TEACHINGS TO BE OF A SINGULAR TRUTH AND IN THIS CONCEPT THEY BELIEVE THAT NONE OF OTHERS EXIST IN TRUTH. UNDERSTAND: ALL FORMATS OF THE MEDITATIONS, ALL FORMATS OF THE PRAYERS INDEED HAVE MAINTAINED HIGH DEGREE OF VALIDITY.

DIR: Echo, does meditation aid in the development of psychic abilities?

ECHO: INDEED. UNDERSTAND: AS PREVIOUS STATED: IN THAT OF THE MEDITATION, THERE BE INTROSPECTION OF THE INDIVIDUAL. THAT OF THE REFERENCE "PSYCHISM" THERE BE ALSO INTROSPECTION OF THE ENTITY. THIS THEN CREATE AN EXTENSION OF THE AWARENESS OF SELF AND THIS BE THE FOOTINGS OF THE

DEVELOPMENT OF THAT REFER "ADVANCED PSYCHIC ABILITIES".

DIR: Echo, did Jesus practice meditation the way we know it, with 20 minutes in an altered state of consciousness?

ECHO: INDEED NOT. UNDERSTAND HERE: AS THAT OF THE FORM OF THE NAZARENE IN THAT OF THE TRAVELINGS IN AREAS HERE REFER "PAKISTAN, TIBET, MAYLASIA" HAVE EXPERIENCED MEDITATIVE STATES AND IN THE DEVELOPMENT OF THESE IT CARRY THAT OF MEDITATIVE STATE IN A PERMANENT MANNER.

DIR: So He was in this flowing meditative state, that you referred to, all the time?

ECHO: INDEED SO. UNDERSTAND HERE; THIS MAY BE USED OR NOT USED, TURNED ON OR OFF, AS IT BE.

DIR: Echo, are Mantras helpful in meditation?

ECHO: INDEED. THAT OF A MANTRA BE A NONSENSICAL SOUNDING WORD, ALTHOUGH WORD BE NOT IN DESCRIPTION. AS THIS IN REPETITION TEND OF A CONFUSION OF THE LOGICAL MIND AND RELEASEMENT OF THE NON-LOGICAL MIND. THIS THEN INDEED BE ASSISTMENT TO THAT OF FORMAT MEDITATION. HOWEVER, IN THAT OF PREVIOUS MENTION, BE UNNECESSARY.

DIR: Why then do eastern countries feel that it is necessary to blank the mind?

ECHO: INDEED. AS THE INUIT MEDITATES UPON WHERE THE SEAL WILL APPEAR, THE ASIAN WILL MEDITATE USING A MANTRA OR OTHER DEVICE OF ITS CULTURE.

DIR: So there is no benefit gained by blanking the mind?

ECHO: INDEED. WE DID NOT SAY THERE BE NO BENEFIT GAINED. WE SAY, HOWEVER, IT BE UNNECESSARY. AS PREVIOUS STATED, MEDITATIONS MAY BE PERFORMED IN THE SOUL STATE, IN THE ACTIVE STATE, IN THE PASSIVE STATE. THERE BE A DEPENDENCE HERE UPON THAT OF THE INDIVIDUAL CHOICE AND A MANNER OF THE RESONANCE OF THE INDIVIDUAL.

DIR: Can meditation be considered a natural function?

ECHO: INDEED SO. UNDERSTAND HERE: AS ONE OFFSPRING ENTITY BOY BECOME BORED WITH THAT OF FORMAT SCHOOL, THE ENTITY THEN LOOK TO WINDOW AND ENTER INTO STATE OF MEDITATION REFER NEGATIVELY AS "DAYDREAMING". THIS BE INHERENT, NATURAL CAPABILITY OF ALL ENTITIES. THOSE THAT BE IN THE STOPPING OF DAYDREAMING, THOSE THAT REFUSE THE ACCEPTANCE OF THE RELAXMENT STATE, MEDITATIVE STATE DAILY, ENTER INTO THAT WHICH WE REFER "ILLNESS". THERE BE SUCH AS PHLEBITIS, GASTRITIS, ULCERATIONS OF THE STOMACH, OF THE BOWEL AND OF OCCASION AS THAT REFER "CANCERS" AND THAT REFER "TUBERCULOSISES".

DIR: Echo, if a person were to daydream too much, most of the time, would there be a tendency for him to lose touch with physical reality?

ECHO: INDEED SO. UNDERSTAND HERE: THAT OF WHICH WE SPEAK BE MAINTAINED IN BALANCE.

DIR: Echo, a lot of people think that when they sleep they are relaxing. Is this true?

ECHO: INDEED. UNDERSTAND HERE: INDEED SOME ENTITIES RELAX DURING THAT REFER "SLEEP STATE". HOWEVER, MOST ENTITIES MOVE ABOUT THE SLEEPING PAD IN ALMOST CONTINUOUS MOTION THROUGHOUT SLEEP PERIOD. THIS BE MAINTENANCE OF THE CIRCULATORY SYSTEM AND THAT OF ACTIVITY OF THE MIND, AS THE MIND DO NOT SLEEP AND HAVE NO REQUIREMENT OF SLEEP, MERELY THAT OF THE PHYSICAL BODY.

DIR: Are there certain types of music that can enhance the meditative state?

ECHO: INDEED. THAT OF TONES OF THE SIXTH, BETWEEN HERE SIX AND EIGHT VIBRATORY CYCLES PER SECOND, UTTERED IN A QUIETNESS OR HUSH TONE, AS IT WERE. THAT OF SUDDEN STARTLING SOUNDS BE VEXATIONS OF THE MIND AND CREATE INCREASED TENSIONS WITHIN THE PHYSICAL STRUCTURE OF THE BODY.

DIR: You mention tones from six to eight cycles per second. Six to eight to the human ear does not represent a tone. It can not be heard.

ECHO: INDEED. UNDERSTAND: SIX TO EIGHT VIBRATORY INDEED WILL BE ASSIMILATED. HOWEVER, THAT OF THE HEARD TO THE EARS, INDEED NOT. HOWEVER HERE: THAT OF SIX TO EIGHT VIBRATIONS BE INCLUDED SUBLIMINALLY WITHIN THAT OF THOUGHT IN "RESTFUL MUSICS".

DIR: So this could be set up with a wave form generator?

ECHO: INDEED SO.

DIR: Echo, I am going back to mantras here. "OM", that is supposed to be quite a powerful mantra. What, if it is nonsensical and a mantra has no meaning, then why is "OM" so powerful?

ECHO: INDEED. UNDERSTAND: THAT OF THE REFERENCE "OM" SOUND, BE INDEED CREATING THAT OF A VIBRATORY EFFECT WITHIN THAT OF THE AREA OF THE SOLAR PLEXUS AND THAT OF THE AREA OF A PERCEPTION SECTOR OF THE BRAIN. UNDERSTAND: THERE BE IN EFFECT THAT OF THE SETTING UP OF THE SUBLIMINAL VIBRATION.

DIR: Before we get into specific techniques on meditation, what can one expect to experience in meditation?

ECHO: INDEED. FIRSTLY HERE, THERE BE THAT OF A SENSE, SOMEWHAT, OF LOSS OF BODY, THAT OF THE FEELING OF EXISTING ONLY THROUGH THE EYES, THAT OF A FEELING OF WELL-BEING AND OF A ONENESS WITH ALL THE MOLECULES OF THE UNIVERSE. THIS BE

143

SOUNDING, SOMEWHAT HERE, "AIRY FAIRY". HOWEVER, UNDERSTAND: THOSE THAT HAVE NOT EXPERIENCED, HAVE NO REFERENCE POINTS TO REFER TO. THEREFORE, WE MUST THEN SPEAK IN TERMS OF THOSE THAT HAVEN'T EXPERIENCED.

DIR: Echo, are there any specific types of food which aid meditation?

ECHO: INDEED. AS THOSE FOODS THAT BE ALKALINE WITHIN THE BODY. AS THOSE FOODS THAT CREATE ACIDITY WITHIN THE BODY BE AVOIDED AT ALL COSTS.

DIR: Could you give an example of alkaline foods and acid foods?

ECHO: INDEED. ALKALINE BE SUCH AS CITRUS FRUITS. ACIDIC BE SUCH AS COFFEE, RED MEATS, INDEED MEATS IN ANY FORM.

DIR: Is there any harm to meditation at all?

ECHO: INDEED. THERE BE NO HARM BEYOND THAT AN ENTITY ALLOW THAT OF THE FORMAT OF MEDITATION BE ITS ONLY FORMAT.

DIR: Many people have a fear of losing control and they feel in meditation you are losing control of something. Could you please comment on this?

ECHO: INDEED. RATHER HERE, WE QUERY THOSE ENTITIES: HOW, WHY, WOULD ONE ASSUME THAT IN DEALING WITHIN ONE'S OWN MIND, CONTROL BE LOST. UNDERSTAND: IN THAT OF THE FORMAT MEDITATION AN ENTITY BE IN MAINTENANCE FOREVER IN CONTROL. AN

144

ENTITY DECIDE, THAT WHICH BE CORRECT FOR IT, THAT WHICH BE INCORRECT FOR IT. HOW THEN MAY IT EVER LOSE CONTROL, AND TO WHAT WOULD IT BE RELINQUISHING CONTROL? THIS WE DO NOT UNDERSTAND.

DIR: Well, I have heard of people spontaneously leaving their body in meditation, and when I first started meditating myself, I was afraid of that, of astralling without seeming control.

ECHO: INDEED. UNDERSTAND; THAT OF "INVOLUNTARY" BE MISNOMER HERE, AS THE ENTITY HAS INDEED CREATED THAT OF THE FLOW OF ITS BEING FROM PHYSICAL TO ASTRAL, AND HAVE MERELY THE DESIRE OF RETURN AND IT WILL RETURN. UNDERSTAND HERE: THAT OF THE REFERENCE, ALSO, "SILVER CORD OR UMBILICAL TO THE BODY" BE HERE A MEANS OF RETAINING CONTACT OF THE BODY IN THAT OF THE ASTRAL ADVENTURES. THIS, HOWEVER, BE UNNECESSARY BE MERELY THAT OF THE TRIGGERING OF THE MIND TO MAINTENANCE OF THE BODY.

DIR: When Cliff is in the Deep Trance State, as he is now, is that a meditative state?

ECHO: INDEED SO. UNDERSTAND IN THAT OF THE ATTAINING OF THE DEEP TRANCE STATE, THE FORM HAS LEARNED MEDITATIVE METHODS TO RELEASE ITS BEING AND TO CONTACT AN EXPANSION OF KNOWLEDGE WHICH BE PRESENTED, WE, THE ECHO.

DIR: Echo, sometimes when meditating, the mind goes blank. What happens during that time? Is it anything to be concerned about?

ECHO: INDEED NOT. THERE BE THAT OF A NATURAL OCCURRENCE OF THE HUMAN ANIMAL. UNDERSTAND: BE MERELY HERE THAT OF THE INSTANTANEOUS RELEASE AND RETURN OF THE MIND OF THE BODY. BE OF LITTLE CONCERN.

DIR: Can gemstones and crystals benefit meditation?

ECHO: INDEED SO. UNDERSTAND: EACH PHYSICAL ENTITY IN RELATION OF ITS BIRTHING TIME, PLACE HAVE RESONANCE OF AN AREA OF THE UNIVERSE, THAT BE ALSO IN RESONANCE OF CERTAIN MINERALS, METALS, ETC.

DIR: Is our knowledge at present, like the standard gem knowledge and crystal knowledge, are they accurate, or should there be some updating at some future time?

ECHO: INDEED. OF THE DATING HERE: THAT OF THE GENERAL ANIMAL MAN: INDEED IT BEHOOVE THE ENTITIES.

DIR: Sounds like we could have a whole session on that one!

ECHO: INDEED.

DIR: Echo, would you like to direct a meditative cycle for the people listening to this tape?

ECHO: INDEED. THIS BE FOR THOSE THAT HAVE LITTLE IN INVOLVEMENT OF MEDITATIVE STATES. THEREFORE, WE WILL HERE OFFER THAT OF A RELAXATION AND MEDITATION OF

146

REASONABLE SHORT DURATION: THE ENTITY FIND A POSITION TO SIT, LAY, IN WHICH THERE BE THE LEAST PHYSICAL STRESS UPON THE BODY, THEIR HANDS, LEGS, NECK WELL RELAXED, MUSCLES NOT TIGHTENED HERE. THE ENTITY THEN BREATH IN DEEPLY, DEEPLY ..... EXHALE SLOWLY, SLOWLY, FULLY ...... FEEL HERE IN THAT OF THE CONTINUANCE OF THE SLOW, REGULAR BREATHING PATTERNS, THAT OF THE WARM GLOWING FEELING IN THAT OF THE AREA OF THE FEET ...... FEET BECOME WARM,COZY FEELING. THIS THEN BEGIN MOVING, LIKE A SLOW WAVE, FLOODING OVER THE BODY, TO ANKLES.... SLOW RHYTHMIC BREATHING ..... WARM FEELING, MOVE SLOWLY UP LEGS TO KNEE AREA, AND NOW BECOME A WARM, TINGLY, COZY, COMFORTABLE FEELING ...... SLOW.... RHYTHMIC .... BREATHING.... THE WARM FEELING NOW MOVE UP THE LEGS, INTO THE THIGHS, INTO THE LOWER ABDOMEN.... A WARM FEELING ..... COZY....MOVE UP THE BODY ... INTO STOMACH AREA, AND HERE SWIRL ABOUT ..... RELAXING THE STOMACH .... ALLOWING FOR GOOD DIGESTION ...... SLOW ..... RHYTHMIC BREATHING .....

.... THAT COZY WARM FEELING ...... NOW MOVE UP TO THE
HANDS, TO THE VERY FINGERTIPS... WHERE THERE NOW BE TINGLING, TINGLY FEELINGS... WARM, COZY..STEADY, RHYTHMIC, BREATHING ..... AND MOVE UP TO THE MUSCLES OF THE NECK, MUSCLES OF THE THROAT..BECOMING WARM AND AND RELAXED... ..MUSCLES OF THE

147

FOREHEAD BE RELEASED AND RELAXED
AND THERE BE A SLIGHT PRESSURE
FEELING OF THE CENTER OF THE
THOUGHTS... THOSE FLASH IMAGES, WHICH
APPEAR THERE... AND THIS MAY BE
REPEATED AT ANY TIME IT BE SO
DESIRED...DEEP, RHYTHMIC BREATHING-
NOW THE ENTITY HAS ATTAINED A STATE
OF RELAXATION AND MEDITATION.
AND NOW, IN ORDER THAT THE ENTITY BE
AWARE OF ITS STATE, WE WILL COUNT TO
THE NUMBER FIVE. UPON THAT OF
ATTAINMENT OF THE NUMBER FIVE, THE
ENTITY WILL AWAKEN, COMPLETELY
REFRESHED, RELAXED AND IN A
CONTENTED STATE..ONE..TWO..THE ENTITY
REGAINING FEELING THROUGHOUT ITS
BODY.... THREE-FEELING RETURNING
FASTER NOW, THE BLOOD IS FASTER
COURSING THROUGH THE VEINS ...... FOUR
.... READY TO COME AWAKE, VIBRANT,
RELAXED AND HAPPY .....FIVE...THE ENTITY
AWAKE AND REALIZE IT HAS ATTAINED A
FINE STATE OF RELAXATION, MEDITATION
IN A VERY SHORT PERIOD OF TIME.

DIR: Thank you Echo.

ECHO: INDEED WE BE MOST HAPPY TO ASSIST.

DIR: At this time can you tell me what level of trance
Cliff is at?

ECHO: INDEED. THE FORM OF THE ONE CLIFFORD,
TRANCE STATE L, LEVEL 212,
MAINTAINING.

DIR: Thank You. What exactly is that tingling feeling experienced in meditation?

ECHO: INDEED. HERE BEST BE EXPLAINED AS THAT OF THE CONTROL OF MIND OVER THE BODY.

DIR: Obviously it goes deeper than that, but that's a good enough explanation for now?

ECHO: INDEED SO.

DIR: When the body is in total relaxation, do the feet and hands get cold?

ECHO: INDEED. ON OCCASION. HOWEVER, NOT NECESSARY. INDERSTAND; THE ENTITY MAY CONTROL THE BODY, TO ELIMINATE THAT OF THE SLOWING OF THE BLOOD, AND THEREBY MAINTAIN WARMTH.

DIR: Also, in meditation, there is sometimes the sensation of warmth, or sometimes a cool, prickly sensation. Could you please explain those two things?

ECHO: INDEED. UNDERSTAND: BE ONE AND THE SAME. HOWEVER, THIS BE DUE TO TIMING HERE. AS AN ENTITY IN THAT OF THE ATTAINMENT OF A DEEP RELAXED STATE, THERE MAY BE A STATE OF A PHYSICAL TIREDNESS, AND THEREBY DRAW THAT REFER "COLD PRICKLY FEELING" TO ITS BEING, WHEN THE MIND BECOME IN TOTAL CONTROL OF THE BODY. THE ENTITY HAVE MERELY TO REPROGRAM, AS IT WERE, AND THE PRICKLY

149

FEELING BE REMOVED, SHOULD THIS BE DESIRED.

DIR: I have talked to a few people who say they can't meditate. Whenever they take steps into meditation, they fall asleep.

ECHO: INDEED. INDEED BE THEN MEDITATION.

DIR: They really are meditating?

ECHO: INDEED SO. UNDERSTAND: AS PREVIOUS STATED MEDITATION MAY BE PERFORMED IN WAKEFULNESS, SLEEPFULNESS, ACTIVITY, NON-ACTIVITY. AND AN ENTITY SAY IT CANNOT MEDITATE, IN REALITY IT MEAN, IT DO NOT MEDITATE IN A SPECIFIED MANNER.

DIR: Echo, with regular meditation, would a person find that the average rate of his heartbeat be lowered?

ECHO: INDEED. THAT OF REFERENCE "REGULAR MEDITATION?"

DIR: Meditation ongoing, daily, once a day.

ECHO: INDEED. HERE AN ENTITY MAY INDEED SLOW THE SYSTEM. IF THE ENTITY FIND IT BEHOOVE IT, IN THE SLOWING OF THE SYSTEM, TO ASSIST IN RELEASEMENT OF THE MIND.

DIR: Is there a specific heart rate that is favorable, beneficial, for a person to maintain his relaxation?

ECHO: INDEED NOT. UNDERSTAND: BEYOND THAT OF THE GENERAL PHYSICAL PARAMETERS DEALING WITH THAT OF THE HEARTBEAT, UNDERSTAND: MEDITATION BE OF THE MIND

AND IT BE NOT NECESSARY OF THE SLOWING OF THE SYSTEM, ALTHOUGH IT MAY BE PERFORMED.

DIR: There are schools that say one should meditate twice daily, morning and evening.

ECHO: UNDERSTAND: FIRSTLY: ONE NEED NOT A SCHOOL IN ORDER OF THE LEARNING OF ITS OWN BEING. SECONDLY: WHEN AN ENTITY OFFER TO YOU THAT TERM "SHOULD", UNDERSTAND: THERE BE MANIPULATION OF SELF.

DIR: A lot of people come to me after meditation classes, and this be a couple of weeks after, and say: "Every time I want to meditate, the kids start hollering or the cat comes into the room, or the telephone rings, or the kids down the block start yelling, or some other happenings." Why is it that it always seems this type of thing happens?

ECHO: INDEED. UNDERSTAND: IT BE AS THAT OF THE MEDITATION THERE BE THE DRAWING OF THE ENERGIES, FORCES ABOUT THEIR BEING. THIS THAN TEND TO ATTRACT OTHERS ON THAT OF A SUBCONSCIOUS FRAME. THAT REFER CAT HERE, BE HIGHLY SENSITIVE, INDEED ALSO HERE THAT OF YOUNG OFFSPRINGS.

DIR: Quite often it is considered the person wanting to meditate as being selfish.

ECHO: INDEED. WE OF THE ECHO AGREE WHOLEHEARTEDLY, THAT AN ENTITY IN

DEALING WITH SELF, BE IN TOTALITY OF SELFISHNESS. UNDERSTAND: THIS WORD "SELFISHNESS" BE A POSITIVE WORD, HAVE BE CONSTRUED IN YOUR SOCIETY, NEGATIVE.

DIR: So taking this time for oneself is not a negative selfishness?

ECHO: INDEED NOT. WHY THEN WOULD ONE ASSUME, THAT ANOTHER MAY SAY TO IT: "YOU HAVE NOT, MUST NOT, TAKE TIME FOR SELF". THIS BE INDEED STRONG JUDGMENT OF ANOTHER.

DIR: Echo, would you like to say anything in closing?

ECHO: INDEED. FIRSTLY HERE: ADVISEMENT BE: DO NOT BE CAUGHT IN THAT OF THE UNDERSTANDING THAT MEDITATION MAY ONLY BE PERFORMED IN TOTALITY OF QUIETNESS AND IMMOBILITY. IT MAY BE PERFORMED REGARDLESS OF THE MOVEMENT OF THE PHYSICAL OR ACTIVITY OF THE MIND.

DIR: Thank You for this session, Echo.

ECHO: WE OF THE ECHO THANK YOU FOR THE OPPORTUNITY OF APPROACH, THEREFORE WE SAY TO YOU.... GO IN PEACE....
GO IN LOVE…
AND-UNDERSTANDING
WE RELEASE THE FORM.

Chapter 9   Imagination - Creating your reality

Dir: Echo, we would like to discuss imagination today. Do you have an opening statement?

ECHO: INDEED. FIRSTLY, HERE UNDERSTAND: THAT REFER "IMAGINATION" BE THAT OF THE USE OF THE MIND IN DEVELOPMENT OF IDEAS, OF THE RELAXATION, OF THE RESPITE OF THAT OF THE PHYSICAL REALM. ALSO HERE IT BE THAT IN THAT OF THE LEARNING, OF THE BUILDING, OF THE IMAGINATION, AN ENTITY MAY USE THIS FORMAT TO ACHIEVE THAT WHICHSOEVER IT DESIRE.

DIR: Most people find imagination a handicap, rather than a tool. People, whenever their imagination is exercised, other people will say to them...

ECHO: INDEED. FIRSTLY HERE: WHY, IN THAT OF THE DEALING OF THE MIND WITHIN, WOULD AN ENTITY THEN ACCEPT THE JUDGMENT OF OTHERS, WHO HAVE NO REFERENCES TO JUDGE THAT MIND?

DIR: Well, change that: People without imagination far outnumber those with and they have a very ....

ECHO: NOT TRUE. NOW IT BE OF ALL ENTITIES MAINTAIN THAT REFER "IMAGINATION". HOWEVER, SOME ENTITY REFUSE HERE THE

USE THEREOF. THESE ENTITY THEN ALLOW
SELVES THE ENTERING OF THE STATE REFER
"MAINTENANCE OF THE STATUS OF PRESENT".

THOSE IN USE OF IMAGINATION INDEED BE
THOSE THAT EFFECT CHANGE WITHIN THE
PHYSICAL WORLD. THOSE ENTITY, SUCH AS
HIPPOCRATES, SUCH AS ALL THE GREAT
THINKERS, GREAT DOERS, BE ONLY IN THAT
FORMAT OF THE GREATNESS DUE TO THE
USE AND THE FREEDOM OF THEIR
IMAGINATION.
UNDERSTAND: THAT WHICH MAY BE
IMAGINED IN THE MIND, MAY SOME
DAY, SOME WAY, BE BROUGHT TO
PHYSICAL REALITY.

DIR: Echo, first of all we say to ourselves: "It is only my
imagination" or "Maybe I imagined it". Could you
comment on this?

ECHO: INDEED. HERE BE BASICALLY THAT OF A
LACK OF TRUST IN THE TALENTS OF SELF. IT BE
ALSO THAT OF THE ACCEPTANCE OF THE SOCIAL
JUDGMENT HERE. UNDERSTAND: THAT WHICH OCCUR
WITHIN THE MIND OF AN ENTITY MAY NOT BE REFER
"ONLY MY IMAGINATION", AS THAT REFER
"IMAGINATION" BE THAT OF THE STRONGEST, MOST
POWERFUL OF THE NATURAL TOOLS INHERENT IN
THAT OF THE ANIMAL MAN. FIRST, THERE BE
IMAGINATION. SECONDLY, THERE BE THOUGHT
PROCESS APPLIED TO THAT WHICH BE IMAGINED.
THIRDLY, THERE BE THAT OF THE BUILDING,
PHYSICALLY, TO BRING THE IMAGINATION TO
PHYSICAL REALITY. THERFORE, HERE UNDERSTAND:
IMAGINATION BE THAT OF THE MOST POWERFUL OF
THE TOOLS INHERENT IN THAT OF THE ANIMAL MAN.

154

DIR: Some people say to me, especially on courses and things like that, that they do not internally visualize. They don't see pictures in their mind.

ECHO: INDEED. UNTRUE. IT BE MERELY, THAT THESE ENTITY BE FOCUSSING ENTIRELY IN THAT OF THE LOGICAL ASPECTS. THESE SAME ENTITY HERE OFFERED THAT OF THE SOLUTION... CORRECTION, OFFERED THAT OF THE PROBLEM OF MATHEMATICAL RESONANCE: THESE ENTITY THEN, MENTALLY, VIEW THE NUMBERS AND THE SOLUTION. IT BE MERELY THAT THESE ENTITY BE FOCUSSED IN LOGIC AND HAVE DIFFICULTY IN THE FREEING OF IMAGINATION. HOWEVER, IN THAT OF A DESIRE HERE, FREEING OF THE IMAGINATION MAY INDEED BE ACCOMPLISHED.

DIR: Is imagination a conscious or subconscious phenomenon?

ECHO: INDEED. THERE BE THAT OF BOTH HERE. IT BE THAT OF THE EMANATION OF THE SUBCONSCIOUSNESS OF THE ENTITY. THIS BE THAT OF REASONING AS THOSE DEALING IN A PURELY LOGICAL FORMAT FIND DIFFICULTY HERE, AS THAT OF THE SUBCONSCIOUS FREEDOM BE SOMEWHAT SUPRESSED.

DIR: So, is there such a thing as illusionary imagination?

ECHO: INDEED SO. UNDERSTAND; THAT OF THE FREEING OF THE MIND, OF THE THOUGHT PROCESSES, WILL INDEED BRING ABOUT THAT REFER HERE "WANDERING THOUGHT". THIS THEN BE ALSO

155

IMAGINATION. HOWEVER, THE ENTITY HERE WILL DISCOVER SOME SEEPAGE OF THAT REFER "SUBCONSCIOUS DIRECTION".

DIR: Echo: How do hallucinations enter into this? These seem to be real happenings, and yet i is only imagination.

ECHO: INDEED. THAT OF THE HALLUCINATION THERE BE THAT OF MALFUNCTIONS IN THAT REFER "PITUITARY, PINEAL GLANDS." EXCRETIONS HERE OF THE FLUIDS, TOXINS, THAT AFFECT THE MIND AND TRIGGER HERE THE THOUGHT PROCESSES BEYOND THAT OF REFERENCE "HEALTHY MIND"

DIR: How can one tell when he is experiencing an hallucination?

ECHO: INDEED. THE ENTITY THEN PUT THIS TO TEST. DO IT FEEL THIS MAY THEN BE BROUGHT TO PHYSICAL REALITY WITH EFFORT, ET CETERA OR INDEED IT BE MERELY THAT OF A FANCY, AS IT WERE.

DIR: Many people have seen ghosts and feel that they have been hallucinating.

ECHO: INDEED. HERE WE COME TO THAT OF A NEW PANDORA'S BOX.

THAT OF THE PHENOMENON REFER "GHOST" INDEED BE THAT OF THE VIEWING OF-THOSE IN SPIRITUAL PLANE. HOWEVER, HERE IT BE THAT THE ENTITY OF THE PRECISE SECOND HAVE CREATED A FREEDOM OF THE MIND, OF THE

156

SUBCONSCIOUS AND THE CONSCIOUSNESS AT ONCE AND THE SAME TIME, TO FACILITATE THE OPENING TO A SPIRITUAL REALM. THIS BE NEITHER THAT REFER "IMAGINATION" OR "HALLUCINATION". IT BE THAT OF THE REALITY OF THE VIEWING AS ANY PHYSICAL BEING THAT HAVE OBSERVED THIS PHENOMENON WILL TELL YOU. IT REMAIN IN THE MIND, FRESH AND PRECISE, FOR YEARS UPON YEARS AND THIS BE NEITHER HALLUCINATORY OR IMAGINATORY.

DIR: How can one consciously direct the imagination, while freeing the mind simultaneously?

ECHO: INDEED. THAT OF THE FORMAT "MEDITATION" BE FINE FORMAT HERE. UNDERSTAND: IN THAT OF THE RELAXING OF THE CONSCIOUS MIND, THERE BE THEN MORE FREE FLOW OF THE SUBCONSCIOUS MIND AND THE ENTITY, IN MAINTAINING CONSCIOUSNESS, WILL VIEW WITHIN ITS MIND, VIEW, SENSE, FEEL THOSE EMANATIONS OF THE SUBCONSCIOUS. IT MAY THEN HERE DISCOVER THERE BE HIGH DEGREE OF CREATIVITY AVAILABLE TO IT.

DIR: The difference between - I don't know how much that is - between spontaneous imagery and purposely created imagery, is there a difference, and if so, could you please explain it?

ECHO: INDEED. THAT OF COMPARATIVE DIFFERENCE HERE BE MERELY IN THE FORMAT OF ATTAINMENT. WHEN ONE SET FORTH TO ATTAIN, THIS BE ONE FORMAT.

OTHERS MERELY BE THAT OF THE IMPRESSION UPON THE CONSCIOUS MIND OF THAT SUBCONSCIOUS MESSAGE, AS IT WERE.

DIR: Does spiritual guidance influence our imagination?

ECHO: INDEED, SOMEWHAT. UNDERSTAND, HOWEVER: AN ENTITY IN THE PHYSICAL. REALM MAINTAIN TOTALITY OF FREE CHOICE WITHIN ITS THOUGHT PROCESSES WITHIN ITS ACCEPTANCES OF WHICHEVER OCCUR WITHIN.

DIR: Some people have the ability to create imagery with their eyes open, as opposed to most people with their eyes closed. Could you comment an that, please?

ECHO: INDEED. THIS BE MERELY, THAT THESE ENTITIES HAVE THAT REFER HERE "CONCENTRATION", IN WHICH THEY CAN ALLOW THAT OF BOTH COINCIDING HERE: THAT OF THE CONSCIOUS INTAKE OF EYES AND AT ONCE AND THE

SAME TIME THAT OF THE IMAGERY TO ONE SIDE, AS IT WERE, WITHIN THE MIND.

DIR: Echo, that's what happens to me. Only I find it difficult to visualize with my eyes closed.

158

ECHO: INDEED. THEN, BY ALL MEANS, REMAIN WITH EYES OPEN.

DIR: Why would there be that difficulty?

ECHO: INDEED. IT BE HERE MERELY THAT OF THE INDIVIDUAL MAKEUP, AS IT WERE, THAT OF EACH ENTITY PROGRAMMING THROUGHOUT ITS EXISTENCES. THAT OF THE PRESENT PHYSICAL PROGRAMMING OF THE PRESENT CARNATION MAY LEAD AN ENTITY TO THAT OF RESTRICTION OF ITS SUBCONSCIOUS. THAT OF SUCH THINGS AS FEAR OF THE DARK MAY HERE ENTER. THAT OF SUCH THINGS AS "CHILDREN SPEAK ONLY WHEN SPOKEN TO" MAY HERE AFFECT. THAT OF SUCH THINGS AS "BIG BOYS DON'T CRY" OR LITTLE GIRLS DON'T TALK LIKE THAT" MAY BE TRIGGERS, SCARS, AS IT WERE, THAT AFFECT AN ENTITY UPON THAT OF ATTAINMENT OF ADULTHOOD AND THERE BE RETENTION OF THESE SCARS, THAT CREATE RESTRICTIONS WITHIN THE SUBCONSCIOUS OF THE ENTITY.

DIR: Zen Buddhism, and probably other philosophies that do this too, put a great deal of emphasis on the ability to visualize with the eyes open, as though it increases the intensity of the visualization, the drawing power of creating reality, could you please comment on that?

ECHO: INDEED. UNDERSTAND: THAT OF ANY STOLID FORMAT, INDEED THEN BE FINE FOR THOSE THAT HAVE WRITTEN, DESCRIBED THESE FORMATS. HOWEVER, HERE UNDERSTAND: IT BE THAT OF THE

DEALING OF THE INDIVIDUAL MIND IN THE UNDERSTANDING, THAT OF EACH INDIVIDUAL BE THAT OF THE SUM TOTAL OF ITS PAST, OF ALL OCCURRENCES OF THAT PARTICULAR ENTITY. THEREFORE, UNDERSTAND: NO ONE RESTRICTIVE... CORRECTION, NO ONE FORMAT WILL INDEED BE EFFECTIVE OF ALL ENTITIES.

DIR: What is the difference between reality and illusion in relation to the imagination? How is one to know what is real and illusionary?

ECHO: INDEED, UNDERSTAND, AS PREVIOUS STATED: THAT OF THE TESTING HERE WILL SHOW ENTITY. THAT OF A CAREFUL EXAMINATION OF THAT WHICH HAVE OCCUR WITHIN THE IMAGINATION. THERE BE THIS PROBABLE, THERE BE THIS POSSIBLE, THERE BE THIS IMPOSSIBLE. THE ENTITY THEN JUDGE HERE FOR ITSELF. IT THEN CAST OFF THAT WHICH IT DEEM PERHAPS IMPOSSIBLE AND WORK TOWARD THAT WHICH IT DEEMS PERHAPS POSSIBLE.

DIR: Echo, people remember incidences differently from other and disagreements often result. What is the cause of that?

ECHO: INDEED. JUDGMENTALISM.

DIR: Judgmentalism?

ECHO: INDEED. UNDERSTAND: THAT OF FORMAT "ARGUMENT" BE DIRECT RESULT OF AN ENTITY FEELING THE NEED OF THE PROVING OF ITS POINT TO ANOTHER.

DIR: Then why do they remember things differently?

ECHO: INDEED. WE MEAN THAT OF A DIFFERENT VIEWPOINT. UNDERSTAND EACH ENTITY EXIST IN A SEPARATE UNIVERSE, IN A MANNER OF SPEAKING. THERE BE TWELVE ENTITY IN A CIRCLE VIEWING A LARGE ROCK IN CENTER. THAT ROCK MAY BE VIEWED BY ONE PLACING IT AS A PARTICULAR SHADE, SHAPE AND COLOUR. THAT OF THE TWELVE IN CIRCLE WILL EACH VIEW A DIFFERENT ROCK, A DIFFERENT SHAPE, A DIFFERENT COLOUR, MERELY DUE TO THE LOCATION AND THEIR PARTICULAR PERCEPTION.

DIR: So, in other words, we create our own reality through our imaginations?

ECHO: INDEED SO. UNDERSTAND: THERE BE THOSE IN EXISTENCE, THAT UPON CONFRONTATION OF NEGATIVE OCCURRENCES, NEGATIVELY VIEWED OCCURRENCES WITHIN THEIR EXISTENCE, THESE ENTITY TURN THEIR EYES AND THEIR MIND, AS IT WERE, TO THAT UNDERSTANDING, THAT THIS NEGATIVE OCCURRENCE DO NOT EXIST.

DIR: Echo, when we create with our imagination, are we actually creating or are we attracting and drawing to us something that already exists?

161

ECHO: INDEED. UNDERSTAND: ALL THINGS EXIST FOREVER. THAT OF THE USE OF THE IMAGINATION BE AKIN TO THAT OF THE PHYSICALLY BUILDING OF A BOX, ET CETERA. HOWEVER, THIS BE IN THAT OF THE REALM OF THEIR ENERGIES. THOUGHTS THERE BE INDEED REAL, AS INDEED A WOODEN BOX BE REAL. IT BE MERELY OF THE COMMITTING TO THE ATMOSPHERE, AND IDEA THAT WILL THEN ATTRACT THE NECESSARY PARTICULARS TO ASSIST THE ENTITY IN THE FURTHERANCE OF THE IDEA.

AS WITH THAT OF PRAYER, IT BE INDEED ONE AND THE SAME. IN PRAYER, AN ENTITY USE ITS IMAGINATIVE POWER TO EXTEND A WISH TO THAT REFER "GOD" AND TO HAVE THIS WISH FULFILLED.

DIR: So, it almost suggests, that philosophy and imagination are related in some way?

ECHO: INDEED SO. UNDERSTAND: THAT OF THE REFERENCE HERE "MODERN SCIENCES" HAVE MAKE EFFORT OF THE ISOLATION OF EACH FACET OF THE HUMAN MENTAL AND PHYSICAL CAPABILITY. UNDERSTAND HERE: IT BE ADVISED OF THESE ENTITY, RATHER THAN SEPARATING, THAT OF THE JOINING AND THEREIN THE UNDERSTANDING BE AVAILABLE.

DIR: There was an inventor, several decades ago, by the name of Nicola Tesla. He had very, very concrete visionary abilities, in which he actually constructed prototypes and actually tested them in his mind over a period of time. Was his ability special in any way or can anyone come to achieve that type of concrete vision?

ECHO: INDEED. UNDERSTAND: THAT OF THE FORM HERE "TESLA": THIS ENTITY ENCOUNTER THIS SKILL AT THAT OF THE AGE OF APPROXIMATE SIX YEARS. THE ENTITY THEN BE ENCOURAGED, RATHER THAN DISCOURAGED, AND HERE HAVE THE ABILITY OF THE UNDERSTANDING OF THAT WHICH BE OCCURRING WITHIN IT'S MIND,
IN THAT OF THE REFERENCE HERE "NORMAL FORMAT", AN ENTITY, OFFSPRING BE DISCOURAGED GREATLY IN THAT OF THE USE OF ITS MENTAL CAPABILITIES. HERE AN ENTITY MAY INDEED BUILD THESE CAPABILITIES, MERELY THROUGH THAT OF THE FREEDOM OF USAGE.

DIR: Many time I have heard people say that they get their best ideas in dreams.

ECHO: INDEED. HERE THAT OF REFERENCE HERE, THAT OF "DAILY GARBAGES" BE HELD AT BAY IN THAT OF THE FORMAT SLEEP AND RELEASEMENT OF THE SUBCONSCIOUS THEN BE EFFECTED.

DIR: Is daydreaming and sleep dreaming the same and what are the differences if they are not the same?

ECHO: INDEED. MERELY THE DIFFERENCE HERE THERE BE THAT OF CONSCIOUS STATE AND THAT OF SLEEP STATE. THAT OF THE SUBCONSCIOUS HAVE NO REQUIREMENT OF SLEEP.

DIR: OK. You mentioned that the secret --- we will use that word for lack of a better one at the moment--- the secret of creating your reality through imagery was to free the mind. Now you have mentioned meditation.

What step-by-step could a person begin from scratch, so to say, and begin to really realize and be aware that they do create their own reality through imagery?

ECHO: INDEED. HERE FIRSTLY UNDERSTAND: THAT OF THE REFERENCE "FREE THE MIND" DO NOT MEAN THAT OF ALLOWING THE MIND TO BE BLANK AND USELESS. RATHER HERE, IT BE THAT OF A FREEDOM WITHIN A THOUGHT PATTERN TO VIEW, UNDERSTAND AND JUDGE FOR ITSELF, THAT WHICH BE OCCURRING WITHIN THE INDIVIDUAL.

HERE: FIRSTLY, THOSE IN BEGINNINGS HERE FIND A LOCATION OF QUIETUDE, WHERE ONE WILL NOT BE DISTURBED. THEN FIND A POSITION OF THE BODY, THAT BE ENTIRELY COMFORTABLE AND MAY BE MAINTAINED MOSTLY MOTIONLESS A REASONABLE LONG DURATION. HERE "LONG" BE THAT OF A HALF HOUR TO FORTY OF MINUTES. THERE THE ENTITY THEN SIT QUIETLY, PAY CLOSE ATTENTION TO THAT WHICH BE OCCURRING WITHIN THE THOUGHT PROCESSES. HERE ADVISEMENT BE THAT OF MAINTENANCE OF PEN AND PAPER BENEATH THE HAND AND THE ENTITY WRITE HERE THAT OF *ALL* THOUGHTS AND OCCURRENCES AS THEY OCCUR.
UNDERSTAND HERE, HOWEVER: THE ENTITY WILL DISCOVER THAT AS IT BE WRITING ONE THOUGHT, THERE BE MANY OTHERS

164

FLITTING THROUGH THE MIND. THE ENTITY THEN WILL LEARN TO DECIPHER THAT WHICH BE OCCURRING, AS OFTTIMES IT OCCUR IN THAT OF SYMBOLIC PICTURES, WORDS, NUMBERS. THIS BE A BEGINNING FORMAT.

THE ENTITY CARRY THIS FOR THAT OF A PERIOD OF SEVERAL DAYS. IT THEN FIND THAT IT RELAX AND HAVE NOT NEED OF PENCIL AND PAPER AND IT FIND MORE CLARITY WITHIN THAT WHICH BE OBSERVED WITHIN THE MIND. THIS THEN BE GRADUAL BUILDING ....

DIR: Is all well with the form?

ECHO: INDEED

        .... UNTIL THE ENTITY FIND THIS BE IN HIGH DEGREE OF ASSISTMENT IN THAT OF THE USE OF THE IMAGINATION.

DIR: How does one learn to translate their own symbols?

ECHO: INDEED. A FINE METHOD HERE BE THAT OF THE WRITING OF THE SYMBOLS, AND WRITING OF ALL THINGS WHICH COME TO MIND IN ASSOCIATION OF THIS SYMBOL. THE ENTITY THEN READ ALL SYMBOLS. THAT WHICH STAND OUT TO THE ENTITY BE THEN THAT WHICH BE CORRECT OF THIS PARTICULAR OCCURRENCE. UNDERSTAND: AS EACH OCCURRENCE WILL BE PRESENTED SOMEWHAT DIFFERENTLY. HOWEVER, SIMILAR SYMBOLS MAY BE USED. HERE THEN UNDERSTAND: EACH OCCURRENCE OF

A SYMBOL MAY HAVE A DIFFERENT MEANING.

DIR: Echo, how do belief systems affect imagination?

ECHO: INDEED. VERY STRONGLY.

DIR: Could you elaborate on that, please?

ECHO: INDEED. IF ONE BELIEVE THAT THE DEALING OF THE MIND BE, FOR EXAMPLE, WORKINGS OF THE DEVIL, AN ENTITY WILL THEN TRIGGER, IN ITS OWN BEING, THAT OF THE VISUALIZATION OF THE STRANGE FACES, FORMS, EYES IN THE DARK, ET CETERA. UNDERSTAND: THIS BE A BASIS OF THE BELIEF OF THIS ENTITY.

DIR: I see.

PAUSE TO TURN RECORDING TAPE ....

DIR: At this time, can you tell me what level Clifford is at, Please?

ECHO: INDEED.

DIR: Thank You. We have covered up to now mainly what a singular person can do. Now, is it possible to join imaginations of two or several minds to intensify a creativity of a reality?

ECHO: INDEED SO. UNDERSTAND: THIS BE THAT WHICH BE AFFECTED BY THAT FORMAT REFER "GROUP PRAYER". THIS BE THEN THAT OF THE ATTEMPT OF GROUPINGS TO BRING ABOUT ALL THOSE FORCES REFER "GOOD", TO DRAW

166

THOSE FORCES TO THESE ENTITIES FOR THAT REFER "BETTERMENT" OF THEIR EXISTENCES.

DIR: What advice could you give to those seeking, who do it in groups?

ECHO: INDEED. HERE FIRSTLY: THAT OF THE TOTAL REALIZATION OF THE REASON OF THIS PERFORMANCE.
SECONDLY: A REMOVAL OF ALL NEGATIVE WORDINGS AND THOUGHT.

DIR: Basically that's it?

ECHO: INDEED SO.

DIR: Very simple, as are most procedures!

ECHO: INDEED. UNDERSTAND: WHEN ONE SAY: "I WISH FORGIVENESS", THIS BE NEGATIVE, IN THAT AN ENTITY IN THE PHYSICAL REALM BE PERFECT UNTO ITSELF AND THAT OF FORGIVENESS THEN HERE BE THAT OF THE UNDERSTANDING OF PERSONIFICATION OF THE ENERGIES THAT BE.
HERE, THAT OF THE USE OF THE ENERGIES THAT BE, BE AVAILABLE IN POSITIVE.

DIR: Could you clarify that a little? It seems a little confusing.

ECHO: INDEED. AN ENTITY IN THE SENDING, AS IT WERE, FROM ITS MIND, A THOUGHT THAT IS DESIGNED TO RETURN GOOD THINGS TO IT, WILL NOT RECEIVE GOOD THINGS IN SENDING OF NEGATIVE THOUGHT. IT WILL RECEIVE NEGATIVE.

DIR: I see. OK.

Are there any other adjustments one could make, if they were part of a standard religious belief structure, that would enhance their prayers and other outlooks on life, to stimulate creative and positive imagery?

ECHO: INDEED. FIRSTLY: STUDY THAT OF THE POWERS OF THE MIND, AS THIS BE THAT WHICH BE DEALT WITH IN THAT REFER "STRUCTURED RELIGIONS". THAT OF DEVELOPMENT OF UNDERSTANDING OF ITS RELIGION, RATHER THAN THAT OF BLIND ACCEPTANCE THEREOF.

THAT OF THE REALIZATION THAT JUDGMENTALISM BE SELF-DEFEATING, AS THE LAW OF THE UNIVERSE BE: POSITIVE ATTRACT POSITIVE, NEGATIVE ATTRACT NEGATIVE, AND IN THAT OF THE JUDGING OF ANOTHER, THIS BE NEGATIVE.

DIR: Echo, during this entire session, there is a statement that's been running through my mind, from the book "Illusions" by Richard Bach. I don't know how it applies, but: "Argue for your limitations, and sure enough, they are yours".

ECHO: INDEED SO. AS PREVIOUS STATED ONE SAY, "I WISH FOR GOOD THINGS. HOWEVER, I AM NOT WORTHY". THIS THEM BE LIMITATION AND THE ENTITY INDEED BE NOT WORTHY. THEREFORE, GOOD THINGS BE WITHHELD. UNDERSTAND: AN ENTITY THINKING "I CAN'T DO, BECAUSE I AM NOT CAPABLE", BUT THEN DECIDE TO EXTEND THE EFFORT, WILL DISCOVER THAT REFER "FAILURE", AS THE FAILURE HERE BE

PREDETERMINED IN THAT OF THE SUBCONSCIOUSNESS OF THE ENTITY.

DIR: Echo, You talked previously of thought and imagination. I would just like some clarification: are they one and the same, or is there a slight difference?

ECHO: INDEED. THEY BE THAT OF THE SAME. HOWEVER, THERE BE A DIVISION HERE, IN THAT AN ENTITY MAY CONSCIOUSLY CONTROL THOUGHT PROCESSES. IMAGINATION BE THAT OF THE FREEING, RELEASING, AS IT WERE, OF THE STRUCTURED THOUGHT PROCESSES TO ACCESS THAT OF THE UNSTRUCTURED THOUGHT PROCESSES.

DIR: Sometimes, children will have imaginary playmates. Are they real?

ECHO: INDEED. UNDERSTAND HERE, WE COME ONCE MORE, TO THAT OF THE REALM OF THE SPIRIT WORLD. INDEED THESE BE REAL. AS THEY BE THE PERCEPTION OF THE OFFSPRING, THEY BE NOT YET DESTROYED.

DIR: What do you mean by that?

ECHO: INDEED. THAT OF THOSE ENTITY, OF OFFSPRING ENTITY, THAT HAVE PLAYMATES IN SPIRIT REALM.THIS BE DUE TO THAT OF THE PERCEPTION OF THE OFFSPRING ENTITY, THAT THE PERCEPTIVE ABILITIES HERE BE OPEN AND UNDERSTANDING, AND HAVE NOT YET BE DESTROYED BY THAT OF THE

PROGRAMMINGS OF ITS SOCIAL ENVIRONMENT.

DIR: What suggestions do you have for parents in bringing up their children, to encourage the use of their imagination?

ECHO: INDEED. THAT THEY BE ENCOURAGED.

UNDERSTAND HERE: IN THAT OF PRESENT SOCIETY, OF WHICH YOU EXIST,OFFSPRING BE GROWN, AS IT WERE, IN A BASICALLY NEGATIVE ENVIRONMENT.
EXAMPLE HERE: A CHILD BE TAKING FIRST STEP AND BE PRAISED HIGHLY BY ALL IN PERCEIVANCE. A FAMILY THEN GO TO A PUBLIC PLACE, A CHILD WALK AWAY, MOVE AWAY AND BE ROUNDLY SCOLDED FOR THAT OF THE USE OF ITS LEGS, WHICH IT HAVE PREVIOUS BE PRAISED HIGHLY. THIS BE NEGATIVE IN NATURE AND HIGHLY CONFUSING.

.

OFFSPRING ALSO BE BROUGHT INTO GROWTH PATTERNS THROUGH THAT OF NEGATIVE PROGRAMMING PRACTICES, SUCH AS: "DON'T DO THIS" "DON'T TOUCH THAT, "A CHILD MUST KEEP ITS PLACE, ET CETERA, ET CETERA, ET CETERA. A SCHOOLING PROGRAM BE DESIGNED TO QUELL THE IMAGINATION OF THE ENTITY AND TO LEAD THE ENTITY INTO PRESCRIBED FORMAT OF SUBSERVIENCE WITHIN SOCIETY.

170

ADVISEMENT OF THE PARENTS HERE BE
APPROACH CHILDREN IN LOVE, RATHER
THAN ANGER.

DIR: Echo, the school system being what it is, and a
parent who is understanding of how limiting
school can be, how can they help their child
grow?

ECHO: UNDERSTAND HERE: FIRSTLY: THAT OF
PARENTHOOD BE OF HIGHEST
ACCEPTANCE OF RESPONSIBILITY WITHIN
LIFE OF ANY PHYSICAL ENTITY. THERE BE
NO HIGHER DEGREE OF ACCEPTED
RESPONSIBILITY. THOSE ENTITY, PARENTS,
IN AWARENESS WILL NOT ACCEPT A
FORMAT OF RESTRICTIVENESS AND THESE
ENTITY WILL FIND THAT REFER "ANOTHER
WAY".

DIR: I have seen children very much alone in a
classroom of other children, because they
think differently.

ECHO: INDEED SO: UNDERSTAND HERE: WHY
THEN PLACE THIS CHILD WITHIN THIS
ENVIRONMENT?

DIR: Sometimes finances have a lot to do with it.

ECHO: INDEED. THAT OF THE SOCIAL ORDER
AS WELL. HOWEVER, HERE DO
UNDERSTAND: WE DO NOT SAY TO YOU
THAT WE HAVE A PANACEA FOR YOUR
DIFFICULTY.

171

DIR: OK. Echo, how much longer would you suggest this session last?

ECHO: INDEED. THE FORM HERE BE GAINING RAPIDLY IN RIGIDITY AND ADVISEMENT BE THAT OF APPROXIMATE TWO MINUTES HERE IN TIME, IN TIME AS YOU KNOW IT.

DIR: We have a poster, and on the poster it says:

"If you can imagine it, You can achieve it". Would you like to have a closing comment on that?

ECHO: INDEED. BE THIS NOT THE

THEME   OF   OUR   PRESENT

DISCUSSION?

DIR: Yes.

ECHO: WE   HAVE   HERE

REPEATED   AND

REPEATED   THAT

FORMAT. A MIND BE

THAT OF THE MOST

POWERFUL TOOL.
THE IMAGINATION BE THAT FORCE WHICH TRIGGER THE MIND THEN TO ACTION.

THERE BE THAT OF THREE STEPS TO THE BUILDING IN REALITY:

1. THERE BE THAT OF THE IMAGINING OF AN IDEA, THAT OF THE MANIFESTING OF A THOUGHT WITHIN THE IMAGINATION OF AN ENTITY.

2. THERE BE THEN THE JUDGMENT AND THE BUILDING WITHIN THE CONSCIOUS THOUGHT PROCESSES OF THE ENTITY.

3. THERE BE THEN THE BRINGING INTO PHYSICAL RESONANCE THROUGH THAT OF A PHYSICAL ACTION OF THE ENTITY.

   UNDERSTAND HERE: THAT OF THE SOMEWHAT CORNY SAYING HERE:

   IMAGINATION BE BROKEN DOWN TO IMAGES – IN-ACTION

DIR: Thank You for this session, Echo.

ECHO: INDEED. WE OF THE ECHO THANK YOU OF THE OPPORTUNITY OF APPROACH. THEREFORE, WE SAY TO YOU;
GO IN PEACE,

GO IN LOVE AND UNDERSTANDING, WE RELEASE THE FORM.

173

Chapter 10   Spirituality – The Inside Story

DIR: Please clear the mind and indicate when the mind is clear.

ECHO: INDEED SO.

DIR: Please locate and assimilate with the form of your director.

ECHO: INDEED, FORM OF DIRECTOR ---
    ASSIMILATION HERE BE COMPLETE.

DIR: Is all well with the form of Clifford?

ECHO: INDEED. THE FORM OF THE ONE CLIFFORD,
    TRANCE STATE F, LEVEL 521 BROADENING
    NATURALLY.

DIR: Thank you. Echo, this evening we would like to
    discuss spirituality. Most people define spirituality as
    being pure in heart or holy. When one is told he/she is
    spiritual, most likely he/she will deny this. Would you
    please give us your definition of spirituality?

ECHO: INDEED. SPIRITUALITY BE THAT OF THE
    TOTALITY OF UNDERSTANDING OF THAT
    UNIVERSE ABOUT AN ENTITY. UNDERSTAND: A
    SPIRITUAL BEING WILL NOT CREATE, CAUSE,
    PHYSICAL HARM TO ANOTHER, WILL NOT
    CAUSE EMOTIONAL, MENTAL HARM TO
    ANOTHER.
    THIS BE DUE TO THE LEVEL OF
    UNDERSTANDING OF THE SPIRITUAL

175

INDIVIDUAL. IT BE THEN IN REALIZATION THAT IT BE UNNECESSARY OF THE PROVING OF ITS BEING TO ANY OTHER OR/AND OF THE FIGHTING FOR LOVE, AS IT WERE.
UNDERSTAND: SPIRITUALITY TRANSCEND THAT OF A PERSONAL, A MUNDANE. SPIRITUALITY MAY THEN BE DEFINED AS ONE BE KNOWING.

DIR: So a knowing person is a spiritual person?

ECHO: INDEED. THAT OF A TRUE KNOWING INDIVIDUAL INDEED BE SPIRITUAL.

DIR: Echo, how is spirituality connected with the physical?

ECHO: INDEED. IN THAT AN ENTITY IN THE PHYSICAL REALM MAY LEARN, DEVELOP MORE OF ITS SPIRITUALITY IN THAT OF THE PHYSICAL REALM.
HERE UNDERSTAND: THAT OF THE PHYSICAL EXISTENCE BE LEARNING EXPERIENCE. THE ENTITY HERE BE IN DEVELOPMENT, IN GROWTH, OR INDEED IN NON-DEVELOPMENT AND NON-GROWTH. THIS BE RELATED TO SPIRITUAL FACETS OF THE INDIVIDUAL IN THAT WHICH IT PERFORM, THAT WHICH IT DEVELOP IN THE PHYSICAL PLANE, ALSO HERE BUILD OR DEVELOP THAT OF THE SPIRITUAL PORTION OF THE ENTITY.

DIR: Echo, a person, when becoming more aware of the physical side of his nature, does this inhibit his spiritual growth?

ECHO: INDEED NOT. UNDERSTAND: THAT OF THE PHYSICAL AND SPIRITUAL INDEED BE HAND

176

IN HAND. THEREFORE, HERE UNDERSTAND: IN THAT OF OBTAINING OF A HIGH DEGREE OF SPIRITUALISTIC ATTITUDES, AN ENTITY WILL DISCOVER IT BE ALSO HERE BUILDING, GROWING, DEVELOPING IN THAT OF THE PHYSICAL ALSO. INDEED, AS IN THAT OF THE SPIRITUAL AND PHYSICAL, THESE *BE* DEVELOPED TOGETHER.

AN EXAMPLE HERE: AN ENTITY ASSUMING ITS BEING TO BE OF THE SPIRITUAL NATURE. THIS ENTITY THEN DECIDE THAT REFER "CELIBACY" WILL ASSIST IN ITS SPIRITUAL GROWTH. UNDERSTAND: THIS CAN BE NO FURTHER FROM THE TRUTH, AS THAT OF THE SPIRITUAL AND PHYSICAL DEVELOP HAND IN HAND.

DIR: Progressing a little deeper, Echo, what exactly is the origin of spirituality or the spirit?

ECHO: INDEED. HERE IT BE THAT OF THE EMANATION OF LIFE-SPARK, LIFE FORCE FROM THAT REFER "MOLECULAR-ATOMIC STRUCTURE OF THE UNIVERSE". THIS BE THAT REFER "GOD". THERE BE THAT OF A PRIMARY FORCE FROM WHICH EACH AND EVERY ENTITY, PHYSICAL OR SPIRITUAL, EMANATE.

DIR: Echo, since we began this discussion on spirituality, the room has become very, very thick and heavy, and it's almost difficult to think. Would you comment on this, Please?

ECHO: INDEED. ROOM INDEED BE THICK AND HEAVY, AND IT BE DIFFICULT TO THINK. UNDERSTAND: THIS BE RESULT OF THAT OF THE DEALING OF THAT REFER HERE "SPIRITUALISM" OF THE HUMAN ANIMAL.

WE OF THE ECHO APPROACH HERE GLADLY, AS THIS BE OUR DOMAIN, AND WE HAVE HERE ASSISTANCE, THAT BE EMANATING, MANIFESTING OF EACH ENTITY WITHIN PRESENT SURROUNDINGS, AND THE TOTALITY HERE BE NUMBERING THAT OF APPROXIMATE HERE 5 MILLION OF THE PRESENT.

UNDERSTAND: THERE BE THAT OF THE SPIRIT REALM. CORRECTION HERE.. SPIRITUAL REALM, THERE BE OF A HIGH DEGREE OF ATTRACTION OF THE INTEREST, WHEN IT BE DISCOVERED, THOSE IN THE PHYSICAL PLANE BE OPEN TO DEVELOPMENT OF OUR FURTHER UNDERSTANDINGS.

DIR: For the benefit of those listening to this tape: Normally The ECHO comprises a total of APPROXIMATELY 11,000.
OK. Obviously a popular subject, You mentioned, that when a person wished to open himself to the understanding and awareness of the spiritual, it seemed, that there was always, how shall I say it, spiritual help involved?

ECHO: INDEED, THAT OF AVAILABILITY OF THE HELP, AS IT WERE, BE OMNIPRESENT. HERE UNDERSTAND AS WITH THAT OF THE FORM OF THE ONE CLIFFORD, THIS ENTITY IN THAT REFER "PRIOR YEARS" BE OF A HIGH DEGREE PHYSICAL ACTIVITIES, HIGH DEGREE VIOLENT ACTIVITIES, HIGH DEGREE JUDGMENTALISM. UPON THE DECISION OF THE ENTITY TO OPEN ITS BEING, ITS MIND TO THE FURTHER LEARNINGS AT THAT OF THE AGE OF APPROXIMATE 39 OF YEARS, THE ENTITY THEN DECIDE THAT WE, THE ECHO, HAVING WAITED

178

OF THIS ENITITY THE 39 OF YEARS, THEN HAVE ABILITY, AVAILABILITY OF FURTHER ASSISTING THE ENTITY AND INDEED OF MANIFESTING THROUGH THE ENTITY.

DIR: Echo, could you tell us more in depth, of exactly what a soul is, and also how were individual souls first created?

ECHO: INDEED. FIRSTLY HERE: AS THAT OF PREVIOUS QUERY, IT BE THAT OF THE EMANATION FROM THAT OF ATOMIC STRUCTURE OF THE ATMOSPHERE.
BEYOND THIS, WE MAY NOT DIVULGE.

DIR: May not divulge?

ECHO: INDEED. UNDERSTAND: THAT OF THE ANIMAL MAN, IN ITS PRESENT TECHNOLOGICAL THOUGHT PROCESSES, IN THE LEARNING FURTHER, MAY THEN DESTROY ITS EXISTENCE.

DIR: You mean in learning what this soul is he can destroy himself?

ECHO: INDEED. IN THAT OF THE LEARNING HERE OF THE TECHNICAL ASPECTS OF THE BEGINNING OF THE PRIMARY SOUL, INDEED SO.

DIR: The last half of how our individual souls are created, is that what you are referring to?

ECHO: INDEED SO.

DIR: OK., needless to say, man doesn't need any more information, with which to blow himself up!

ECHO: INDEED SO.   THE ENTITY BE SET UPON A FINELY CONSTRUCTED PATH OF THE PRESENT.

DIR: I don't know what I am trying to deduce here, but you mentioned that, when talking about souls and their origin from the emanations from the atmosphere, you were talking about God. There seemed to be some correlations with the universe and God. What universe are you talking about? The physical universe?

ECHO: INDEED. THERE BE HERE THAT, WHICH BE IN GENERAL TERMS ON PLANET EARTH DESCRIBED UNIVERSE, THAT, WHICH CONSIST OF THE STARS, OF THE PLANETS, ASTEROIDS, OUTER SPACE, OF AIR, EARTH, ET CETERA.

DIR: How does this physical universe relate to spiritual universe or whatever?

ECHO: INDEED. UNDERSTAND HERE: IT BE OF ALL OF ONE AND THE SAME, YOU SAY, AN ENTITY IN THE DEVELOPMENT OF ITS PHYSICAL, MENTAL BEING TO THAT STATE, WHICH BE REFER "SPIRITUAL", YET RETAINING A PHYSICAL, AN ENTITY MAY THEN CONTROL THE ENVIRONMENT ABOUT IT, MAY THEN DEAL WITH THAT REFER "WILD ANIMALS", MAY THEN WALK ON WATER, MAY THEN CAUSE ITS BEING TO DISASSEMBLE AND REASSEMBLE ELSEWHERE, IT MAY THEN DEAL WITH FIRE AND RESTRUCTURE THIS, RESTUCTURE THAT OF THE CLIMATE ABOUT IT. UNDERSTAND: THIS BE ALL ONE AND THE SAME, IT BE A CO-REACTION BETWEEN THE PHYSICAL, SPIRTUAL.

DIR: OK., you speak of what we call miracles and those who have performed them in the past we call spiritual masters and are highly worshipped and revered on the planet. Could you...

ECHO: INDEED. IS THIS NOT AN ERROR, IN THAT OF THE WORSHIPPING OF ANOTHER, RATHER THAN THE LEARNING WITHIN SELF TO PERFORM SAME?

DIR: Now, that we are on the topic of miracles, would you please discuss the role of religion as related to spirituality?

ECHO: INDEED. UNDERSTAND: THAT REFER "RELIGIONS" INDEED HAVE HIGH DEGREE RESONANCE TO THAT REFER "SPIRITUALITY", IN THAT OF THE PERFORMING OF GROUP PRAYERS THIS INDEED BE SPIRITUAL IN NATURE. HOWEVER, WE OF THE ECHO, HAVE HERE SOME DEGREE RESERVATIONS OF THAT OF THE WORDINGS OF PRESENT USAGE PRAYERS. IN THAT OF ALL OF THE WORLD'S RELIGIONS, PRAYERS HAVE BEEN DIRECTED TO CREATE DIFFICULTY OF OTHERS, HAVE BEEN WORDED TO CREATE THOUGHT PROCESSES OF THE PRAYEE, AS IT WERE, TO ENTER WORTHLESSNESS, AS IT WERE. THIS HERE, WE OF THE ECHO BE IN DISAGREEMENT, AS EACH ENTITY BE OF TOTALITY OF WORTHINESS AND THERE BE NOT ANY BEING, THAT MAY SAY TO ANOTHER: "YOU BE LESS".

DIR: Jesus said: "Blessed be the poor in spirit".

ECHO: INDEED SO. UNDERSTAND HERE: THAT BE REFERENCE, THAT THE POOR, HERE MONETARILY OWNERSHIP POOR, BE STILL EVER, ALWAYS BLESSED, AS THE SPIRIT FOREVER BE THAT, WHICH BE OF THE ONE.

DIR: So it doesn't have anything then to do with unworthiness?

181

ECHO: INDEED NOT.

DIR: How about humble? How does that relate to it?

ECHO: INDEED. HERE, ONCE MORE, WE OFFER HERE A QUERY: DO ONE HUMBLE BEFORE ONESELF?

DIR: No, no 1 guess not.

ECHO: INDEED NOT. THERFORE THEN: WHY INDEED THEN WOULD ONE ASSUME, THAT HUMBLENESS BEFORE ANOTHER THEN CREATE SOMEHOW SPIRITUALITY WITHIN?

DIR: Yes, that is a good question? What about ego, then, if we consider ourselves...

ECHO: INDEED.

DIR: ... Worthy of ... How do I put this?

ECHO: HERE DO NOT ASSUME THAT BECAUSE ONE BE SPIRITUAL, IT THEN BE BETTER OR GREATER, THAN ANOTHER. UNDERSTAND THAT OF THE BASIS OF THAT REFER HERE "NEGATIVE EGO" BE THAT OF THE REFERENCE "COMPARATIVE". AN ENTITY MAY NOT DEVELOP A NEGATIVE EGO, IF IT DO NOT COMPARE.

DIR: Interesting. You mention the practice of prayer. First of all, is prayer a worthwhile activity, and if so, how may one best go about it?

ECHO: INDEED. UNDERSTAND: PRAYER INDEED BE A WORTHWHILE ACTIVITY. PRAYER MAY TAKE A FORM, WHICH AN ENTITY DESIRE, MAY BE

PERFORMED IN LARGE GROUPS CHANTING "OM", MAY BE PERFORMED BY AN ENTITY MERELY IN THOUGHT DURING THE COURSE OF NORMAL ACTIVITIES.

IT MAY BE PERFORMED IN THAT OF THE MEDITATIVE OR RELAXED STATE. IT BE HERE THAT OF CHOICE OF AN ENTITY UNDERSTANDING THAT PRAYER BE THE COMMITTING OF THOUGHT TO THE ATMOSPHERE, AS IT WERE, IN THE REALIZATION, THAT THOUGHT INDEED BE REAL. INDEED BE A MANIFESTED ACTIVITY OF THE MIND, AND AN ENTITY MAY THEN DRAW TO IT THAT, OF WHICH IT PRAY.

DIR: These people, when they pray, they are praying to God as the...

ECHO: INDEED. UNDERSTAND HERE: WE HERE DO NOT MAKE THE JUDGMENT OF RIGHT OR WRONG. THAT OF THE FORMAT PRAYER BE OF A HIGHLY USEFUL FORMAT. IN RELATION OF THAT OF THE RELIGIONS IT BE USEFUL, IN THAT MANY ENTITIES HAVE THE OPPORTUNITY OF PRAYER, THAT THEY MAY OTHERWISE NOT USE.

DIR: Jesus prayed to God, to God the Father.

ECHO: INDEED. UNDERSTAND: WE OF THE ECHO PRAY TO GOD, THE FATHER, AS THAT OF THE GOD-BEING, THAT ORIGIN FROM WHICH WE AND THEE EMANATE. THAT OF THE TERM "FATHER" BE SYMBOLIC, RATHER THAN ACTUAL.

DIR: You say you pray. Why would a spiritual being in the spiritual realm need to pray?

ECHO: INDEED. WHY NOT? UNDERSTAND HERE: THAT OF THE SPIRITUAL REALM BE THE SAME AS PHYSICAL REALM, MERELY THAT OF THE PARALLEL PLANE. WE EXIST HERE, YOU EXIST THERE, DO NOT THEN ASSUME, THAT OF THE SPIRITUAL REALM BE BETTER OR GREATER OR DIFFERENT.

DIR: From our point of view, you seem to know an awful lot more than we do in the physical realm. So, there seems to be some advantages?

ECHO: INDEED. (humorously) WE WILL HERE MODESTLY ADMIT SO. HOWEVER, HERE UNDERSTAND: IT BE MERELY HERE THAT OF AVAILABILITY OF A DIFFERENT, OR, REFERENCE, "NON-EXISTENT", TIME SPAN, TIME - RELATIONSHIP. ALSO HERE, WE HAVE THE FREEDOM OF MOVEMENT THAT BE INSTANTANEOUS AND YOU BE FETTERED IN THE PHYSICAL. THEREFORE HERE, DO NOT ASSUME THAT WE OF THE SPIRIT REALM KNOW MORE.
IT BE MERELY A DIFFERENT ANGLE OF PERCEPTION.

DIR: Many people and specifically those of scientific mind, and our scientists of this period, place a great deal of emphasis on proof of spiritualness or spirituality. They are always looking for proofs. Could you comment on this, please?

ECHO: INDEED. THESE ENTITY BE TIED IN THEIR THOUGHT PROCESSES TO THAT OF THE PHYSICAL REALM. THEY HAVE DEVELOPED JUDGMENTALISM TO AN ART AND INDEED, IN THAT OF THE DEALINGS OF THOSE ABSTRACTS THAT MAY NOT BE SEEM OR TESTED, THESE

184

ENTITY HAVE HIGH DEGREE OF DIFFICULTY IN THE UNDERSTANDING.

ALSO HERE, DO NOT BE CAUGHT IN THE TRAP THAT ONE TERMED "SCIENTIST" BE ALSO ONE THAT BE KNOWING OF ALL, AS THIS BE UNTRUE. THIS ENTITY INDEED BE "SCIENTIST". HOWEVER, ONE DEALING IN SPIRITOLOGY MAY INDEED CAUSE THIS ENTITY'S HEAD TO SPIN.

DIR: Echo, how is it, that scientific proof, the intellect, became to be considered superior to the spiritual?

ECHO: INDEED. AND WHO CONSIDER THIS?

DIR: The general public seem to. They look down on anything that is not physical.

ECHO: INDEED. UNDERSTAND: BE HERE A GRADUAL IMPRESSION OF THE MINDS OF THE PHYSICAL ENTITY. THERE BE FIRSTLY HERE THOUGHT PATTERNS OF THAT OF THE MEDICAL PROFESSION OF APPROXIMATELY HERE 400 YEARS PRIOR OF THIS DISCUSSION.

IT BE THAT OF THE BUILDING OF THE SELF-IMPORT AND THE BRANCHING FORTH HERE IN RESEARCHES, STUDIES, THAT THESE ENTITY BE RESPECTED, REVERED TO THE POINT, THAT IN THE PRESENT, IN YOUR PRESENT TIME, THAT REFER TECHNOLOGY THERE BE THE UGLY MONSTER THAT INDEED CONTROL POPULATION OF THE PLANET EARTH.

UNDERSTAND: DUE TO THIS FOLLOWING OF THE FALSE GOD, AS IT WERE, THE PLANET BE NEARING THAT OF DESTRUCTION DUE TO MISMANAGMENT, MISTREATMENT, GREED AND AVARICE.

185

DIR: Is there any way this can be avoided through spirituality?

ECHO: INDEED. THAT OF THE SPREADING OF THE SPIRITUAL UNDERSTANDING, THAT BE TWO FOLD: THERE BE DEALING WITH THAT REFER "LOVE". THIS BE LOVE FOR ALL, AND THAT OF THE UNDERSTANDING OF PEACE AND THAT, WHICH MAY BE ATTAINED THROUGH PEACE BE OF HIGHER, (COMPARATIVE) DEGREES, THAN THAT WHICH MAY BE ATTAINED THROUGH STATE OF NON-PEACE.

DIR: Is there time enough to change it?

ECHO: INDEED SO.

DIR: Many people, within themselves, feel a yearning, that they can't put their finger on and they go around looking at this organization and that organization and trying to find some external thing that will satisfy this yearning inside of them. Could you please comment, especially on the upsurgence of this internal yearning of mankind?

ECHO: INDEED. THERE BE COMPLEXITIES HERE.

UNDERSTAND: THAT OF THE INNER YEARNINGS OF THOSE SEARCHING BE THAT OF, REFERENCE, HERE, "SUBCONSCIOUS REMEMBRANCES" OF THAT OF THE SPIRITUAL REALM. THERE BE THAT OF THE TIME, WHEN THESE ENTITY BE IN EXISTENCE WITHIN THE SPIRIT REALM, AND THERE BE A DEGREE OF REMEMBRANCE HERE, THAT BE FELT, SOMEWHAT, AS AN IMPENDING FEELING ABOUT AN ENTITY. ALSO HERE IT BE THAT DEEP WITHIN THESE ENTITY THERE BE THAT KNOWING, THAT NOT ALL BE WELL IN THEIR PRESENT EXISTENCE OR IN THEIR PRESENT

ATTITUDES AND IN THEIR PRESENT UNDERSTANDING. THESE ENTITY, UPON THAT OF THE ATTAINMENT OF THE LEARNINGS, OF UNDERSTANDINGS, MAY THEN DELVE TO THAT OF THE SPIRIT REALM...
CORRECTION HERE... SPIRITUAL REALM AND THEN ATTAIN THAT STATE OF THE MENTALITY OF DEVELOPMENT, THAT BE REFER "NIRVANA" "COSMIC "CONSCIOUSNESS" ET CETERA. AN ENTITY, UPON ATTAINING THIS STATE, THEN NO LONGER FEEL THE DESIRE OF WAR, OF ARGUMENTATION, OF ANGERS, OF JUDGMENTALISM OR INDEED, OF THE PROVING OF SELF TO ANOTHER..

DIR: You just said "Spirit Realm", than "correction Spiritual Realm".

ECHO: INDEED SO. HERE BE: WE HAVE WISH TO MAKE THAT OF A DISTINCTION HERE BETWEEN THAT REFER "HIGHER SPIRITUAL REALM" AND "LOWER SPIRITUAL REALM", AS THAT OF LOWER SPIRIT REALM THERE BE THOSE IN THE CROSSING FROM PHYSICAL TO SPIRIT, YET BE IN CONFUSION.

DIR: PAUSE PLEASE. (turning tape over)

Echo, at this time, can you tell me what level the form of Clifford is at, please?

ECHO: INDEED. THE FORM OF THE ONE CLIFFORD, TRANCE STATE "K", LEVEL 9210, MAINTAINING.

DIR: At any time during this session, did Cliff go deeper than that?

ECHO: INDEED SO.

DIR: Would you care to tell me what level that was?

ECHO: INDEED. THE ENTITY HERE BE LOWERED, EXPANDED, TO THAT OF THE "L" STATE, OF APPROXIMATE LEVEL 500, MAINTAINED OF APPROXIMATE 14 MINUTES. HE THEN RETURN TO THAT OF THE "K".

DIR: Thank you. Some people feel that the intellect or the mind is the soul or spirit. Is that correct?

ECHO: INDEED. IN THAT OF A MANNER OF SPEAKING. UNDERSTAND: SOUL BE THAT OF LIFE FORCE OF THE ENTITY. MIND ALSO BE PORTION OF LIFE FORCE. HOWEVER, MIND, MENTAL ACTIVITY, ALSO BE THE PRODUCT OF THE PHYSICAL BEING.

DIR: Echo, does a man's spiritual essence live forever?

ECHO: INDEED SO. ALSO THAT OF WOMEN, ALSO THAT OF CHILDREN.

DIR: Cats and Dogs, too?

ECHO: INDEED. IN AN MANNER, HERE, OF SPEAKING.

DIR: Do psychism and spirituality go hand-in-hand?

ECHO: INDEED SO. UNDERSTAND: THAT REFER "PSYCHISM" BE IN REALITY THAT OF THE USAGE OF THE MIND. THIS, THEN BE INDEED THAT OF THE USE OF THE SPIRITUAL PORTION, FACETS, OF AN ENTITY. UNDERSTAND: RATHER HERE THAN "PSYCHISM", THAT OF THE WORD "SPIRITUALISM" MAY BE SUBSTITUTED.

188

DIR: You mentioned a person attaining Nirvana being on the road or maybe the end of the road of spiritual seeking. Could you explain more about that state and how one may effectively reach it?

ECHO: INDEED. UNDERSTAND IT BE HERE NOT THAT OF THE END OF THE ROAD, AS IT WERE. HOWEVER, AN ENTITY IN THAT OF THE PHYSICAL REALM MAY ATTAIN THAT REFER "COSMIC CONSCIOUSNESS", "NIRVANA", AT ANY TIME, ANY POINT IN ITS EXISTENCE, THAT IT SO DESIRE.
UNDERSTAND HERE: THIS BE NOT THAT OF THE FAR OFF, HARD TO REACH, MOUNTAINTOP OF SPIRITUAL DEVELOPMENT. RATHER, IT BE THAT OF THE ORDINARY, IT BE THAT OF THE DUE OF EACH AND EVERY ENTITY, SHOULD AN ENTITY SO DESIRE.
IN THAT OF ATTAINING HERE, IT BE NECESSARY THAT AN ENTITY MAINTAIN LOVE OF ITS FELLOW MAN.
HERE UNDERSTAND: THIS MEAN LOVE OF THE FELLOW MAN, NOT NECESSARILY A LIKING OF THE INDIVIDUAL. IT HAVE THE REQUIREMENT OF REMOVAL OF JUDGMENTALISM, WHICH INDEED BE A DIFFICULT STEPPING STONE OF THE HUMAN ANIMAL. EVEN THOSE DEALING IN THE SPIRITUAL ASPECTS OF THE ANIMAL MAN BE OF HIGH DEGREE JUDGMENTALISM, SUCH AS SPIRITUAL LEADERS, BELIEVING THEIR WAY IS THE ONLY WAY. THIS BE UNTRUE. THERE BE AS MANY WAYS OF ATTAINMENT AS THERE BE PHYSICAL ENTITIES IN PHYSICAL EXISTENCE.

DIR: That leads us again to western religions. They place a great deal of emphasis on Sin and its subsequent damage to the soul. What do you have to say about this?

ECHO: INDEED. UNDERSTAND: THAT REFER "SIN" BE A SOCIAL JUDGMENT, A SOCIAL REGULATION HERE. IT DICTATE THAT WHICH "SIN" IS.
EXAMPLE: SEXUAL INTERCOURSE IN ONE LAND BE ACCEPTED OPENLY AND NAIVELY, IN ANOTHER LAND, MERE SHOWING OF THE SEXUAL ORGANS WILL RESULT IN INCARCERATION AND AN HIGH DEGREE OF SOCIAL JUDGMENT.
THEREFORE HERE, IN THAT OF THE USAGE OF THE WORD "SIN", FIRST DEFINE THAT WHICH "SIN" BE FOR YOU WITHIN YOUR ENVIRONMENT.

DIR: So what effect do our so-called sins, social or otherwise, have an our souls?

ECHO: INDEED NONE. UNDERSTAND: THE ENTITY BE IN PHYSICAL EXISTENCE IN ORDER THAT IT MAY EXPERIENCE AND FURTHER DEVELOP WITHIN THE MIND, WITHIN THE SPIRIT AND INDEED WITHIN THE SOUL. SHOULD THIS ENTITY DECIDE OF THE MAINTENANCE OF A LEVEL OF UNDERSTANDING, IT INDEED THEN REMAIN AT THAT LEVEL OF UNDERSTANDING.
UPON THE CROSSING TO SPIRITUAL REALM, UPON REBIRTH TO ANOTHER PHYSICAL BEING, THE ENTITY THEN MAY TAKE ITS CHOICE OF FURTHER DEVELOPMENT OR THE MAINTAINING.

DIR: You speak of reincarnation?

ECHO: INDEED SO. WE SPEAK HERE OF THE REALITY OF EXISTENCES.

DIR: Echo, how did the original sin evolve, that we've been brought up with?

ECHO: INDEED. WE DO NOT UNDERSTAND.

DIR: We have been told, that when we are born, we have to be Baptized and Christened, because of the "original sin of man".

ECHO: INDEED. ORIGINAL SIN BEING?

DIR: I'm not even sure. It doesn't seem to be explained. Original sin just suggests that we are bad.

ECHO: INDEED. IN THAT OF REFERENCE HERE, "CHRISTIAN RELIGION", IT BE THAT OF THE ASSUMPTION HERE.THAT OF THE EXAMPLE: ADAM AND EVE CREATE A SIN IN THAT OF THE SEXUAL INTERCOURSE OF THE BODIES.
UNDERSTAND HERE: THIS THEN BE CARRIED THROUGH RELIGIOUS DOCTRINE AS ONE MEANS OF CONTROL OF THE POPULATIONS. IN THAT OF THE ASSUMPTION THAT ENTITIES IN THE PROPAGATION OF THE SPECIES MUST THEN NECESSARILY COMMIT A SIN OF THE BODY, TO BRING FORTH THE SPAWN OF THIS SIN. UNDERSTAND HERE: THAT OF THE SEXUAL INTERCOURSE OF THE BODIES BE ENTIRELY NATURAL AND INDEED MOST BEAUTIFUL. WHY THEN WOULD ONE ASSUME THIS TO BE UGLY, UNSEEMLY OR IMPROPER?

DIR: Echo, does all experience assist spiritual growth, or is there some that would create a state of stagnation?

ECHO: INDEED. STAGNATION BE MAINTAINED IN THAT OF THE ALLOWING OF THE MIND THAT

191

FORMAT REFER "MADNESS" THAT FORMAT ALSO REFER "RETARDATION". THIS BE WITHDRAWAL OF THE SPIRITUAL ENTITY, OR ATTEMPT OF WITHDRAWAL.

DIR: Isn't it all too easy to choose this? You are not saying they are in a state of stagnation, are you?

ECHO: INDEED.

DIR: So they are stagnating, because they are only partially living in the physical? Is that what you mean?

ECHO: INDEED SO.

DIR: Why would they choose this?

ECHO: INDEED. UNDERSTAND HERE: IT BE THAT REFER "ERROR". AS AN ENTITY CHOOSE ITS PARENTS FROM THE SPIRIT REALM, IT THEN ENTER AND BE BORN INTO THE PHYSICAL REALM. HOWEVER, AS IN THAT OF ALL EXISTENCES, THERE BE THAT OF THE "WHOOPS"!

DIR: Why is it, that many mentally retarded seem to be very child-like?

ECHO: INDEED. WE HEAR THAT OF A CONNECTION OF CHILD-LIKE TO SPIRITUAL?

DIR: I am referring to, I guess, Jesus saying: "Be as a little child and you shall enter the kingdom of heaven".

ECHO: INDEED. THIS REFERENCE BE THAT OF THE TRUSTING OF SELF.

DIR: Echo, I am going to go back to what you said about sin. Sin being our social standards. Are you saying then, there is no right or wrong'?

ECHO: INDEED. INDEED, THERE BE NOT THAT WHICH BE RIGHT OR THAT WHICH BE WRONG IN THE ATTITUDES, ACTIONS OF THE PHYSICAL ENTITY, OTHER THAN IT AFFECT THAT OF THE SOCIAL ENVIRONMENT.

DIR: Well, what about killing? That does not seem right to me!

ECHO: INDEED AND THIS INDEED AFFECT THAT OF THE SOCIAL ENVIRONMENT. UNDERSTAND: ONE WILL NOT ALLOW AN ENTITY TO GO ABOUT KILLING WHOMSOEVER IT DESIRE. THIS BE IN OPPOSITION OF THE SOCIAL ENVIRONMENT IN WHICH THE ENTITY EXIST. AND UNDERSTAND: ALL ENTITY HERE HAVE EQUAL RIGHTS, AS IT WERE. AN EXAMPLE: 1 HAVE THE RIGHT TO REMOVE A KILLER FROM MY ENVIRONMENT.

DIR: Yes! Which right is right?

ECHO: INDEED SO.

DIR: In speaking of Nirvana, it reminded me that a lot of the Yogi masters of the east, place a great deal of emphasis on extreme depth of meditation. (I.E.) Nirvana for the purpose of wiping out the need for many re-incarnational existences. Could you please comment?

ECHO: INDEED. UNDERSTAND: AN ENTITY MAY INDEED CHOOSE THIS FORMAT, SHOULD IT SO DESIRE. THIS BE THAT OF THE RELEASEMENT

193

OF THE MIND TO THAT OF THE SPIRITUAL REALM, AND IN THAT OF THE SPIRITUAL REALM, THE ENTITY MAY THEN EXAMINE, EXPERIENCE, ITS EXISTENCES.

DIR: So, when they say in their teachings, that if you learn to reach the "sumani" state, then you will wipe out the need for a lot more physical incarnations on the planet?

ECHO: INDEED, OF SOMEWHAT. WE HERE TAKE EXCEPTION TO THE WORD "NEED".

DIR: Would you care to elaborate on that?

ECHO: INDEED. THERE BE NO NEED OF THE RE-INCARNATIONAL EXPERIENCE. IT BE RATHER THAT OF THE EXERCISE OF THE CHOICE OF AN INDIVIDUAL.

DIR: How much longer would you suggest this session last, Echo?

ECHO: INDEED. THE FORM BE GAINING RIGIDITY RAPIDLY. WE HERE ADVISE THAT OF LESS THAN THREE MINUTES IN TIME, IN TIME AS YOU KNOW IT. WE MUST THEN RELEASE THE FORM.

DIR: OK. Echo, would You care to tell us how one can enhance their spirituality?

ECHO: INDEED. FIRSTLY AS PREVIOUS STATED: LEARN,   DEVELOP   TRUE   LOVE, UNCONDITIONAL LOVE, LIVE IN PEACE AND HARMONY WITH ALL ABOUT YOU. THIS BE ALL OF NECESSITY.

DIR: What is the strongest spiritual force in the universe?

ECHO: INDEED. THERE BE HERE, A COMBINATION HERE: IT BE LOVE IN ACCOMPANIMENT OF UNDERSTANDING.

DIR: So simple!

ECHO: INDEED SO.

DIR: Why does man always seek for a complicated solution?

ECHO: INDEED. IT BE THE NATURE OF THE ANIMAL.

DIR: Echo, do you have a closing statement?

ECHO: INDEED. HERE WE SAY TO YOU: SEARCH NOT OF THE SPIRITUALITY, AS THE VERY SEARCHING DRAWS ONE AWAY. THE REAL SPIRITUALITY BE WITHIN. THEREFORE, OBSERVE CAREFULLY WITHIN. LIVE IN HARMONY, IN PEACE,
REMOVE JUDGMENTALISMS AND DEVELOP THE UNDERSTANDINGS OF YOUR SOCIAL ENVIRONMENT.
AT THIS POINT WE MUST RELEASE THE FORM.

WE OF THE ECHO THANK YOU OF THE OPPORTUNITY OF APPROACH.
THEREFORE, WE SAY TO YOU GO IN PEACE. GO IN LOVE AND UNDERSTANDING. WE RELEASE THE FORM
....

195

Chapter 11   Alcoholism - Another Perspective

Director:
We are going to be discussing alcoholism today. I wonder if you could please give us an opening statement on alcoholism and its cause?

The Echo:
Indeed. Firstly here, understand: That refer alcoholism be an illness of which an entity have an high degree of negative resonance, due to that of sugars. This be expressed by an entity through that of the consumption of alcohol.
Understand: This be that of the physical reasonings of that refer "alcoholism". There be also emotional resonance alcoholism and this be many faceted. An entity may choose a path of alcohol to hide its being, to drown its sorrows, as it were.

Director: You suggested that sugar played a role in alcoholism. Does that mean a person with perhaps low blood sugar or high blood sugar would have more of an affinity towards alcoholism?

The Echo: Indeed. Not necessarily. Only here that of the physical construction of some entity. They be as in resonance with that refer "alcohol" and therefore feel the need of the consumption.

Director:
It has been suggested in some books, that there might be a food allergy against Rye or Hops or something along those lines. Would you agree with that?

The Echo:
Indeed. Understand here, however: It be not possible of the generalization here, as each entity in involvement of the alcoholism be a singular case. That of attempting of the setting of a single cure, as it were, be akin to that of the prisoner attempting of the removal of the stone wall with that of a spoon.

Director: Is there any specific nutritional deficiency, that can generally be related to alcoholism?

The Echo:
Indeed. Rather than a deficiency, that of the overusage of the refer "sugars" and sugar content foods. Understand: Of some entities that of the tolerance of that refer sugars be manifest in requirements of further sugars and this be manifest, in reality, in that of a single, reference here, "ounce" of alcohol consumption, react negatively upon that body.

Director: Are you saying then, that alcohol reacts in the body somewhat the way sugar does?

The Echo:
Of some entity.

Director: So this creates a craving for sugar, when they are not drinking? Is this what you mean?

The Echo: Indeed.

Director:
Alcohol itself is created from sugar by the fermentation process. So therefore sugar and alcohol have similar resonances. Is that true?

The Echo:
Indeed so. Understand: With that of the fermentation, with that of becoming alcohol, it then be of stronger resonance within that of the physical body. An entity that be emotionally unable of coping with it's life format, then find an necessity of the hiding, as it were, in that of alcohol.

Director: You mentioned that alcoholism is an illness. How does it..........

The Echo: Indeed. As previous stated, of some entity the physical construction be in non-resonance and this be construed here "illness". An entity have needs of the ingestion of alcohol and this, in effect, be that refer "vicious circle".

Director: What then is the physical construction that creates the tendency to alcoholism?

The Echo:
Indeed. There be that of the entity maintain requirement within physical structure of the body, that of input of high levels of sugars. The entity then find these levels attained in that refer alcohol. Upon the first ingestions of alcohol, these entities then find "better feelings" within the body. This be, however, of short durations. It be, in effect, the body lying to the mind and the mind then assume that of the use of more alcohol create better feelings. This then, become that refer "vicious circle".

199

Director:
Echo, I still don't understand. Why would one physical construction be non-resonant in the first place, with sugar?

The Echo:
Indeed. Understand: Here it be merely that an entity, upon entry of that of the physical realm be fed in this manner or that manner, dependent upon its environment, its parents, et cetera. There be then a resonance constructed within the body for such things as sugars, meats, vegetables and such.

Each entity in its adjustments within its body develop certain affinities, that it may change from time to time, do it so desire. However, of the changing format, require also that of the advanced thought processes; and there be some entity, without here expressing judgmentalism, it be some entity indeed use mind of little.

Director:
Basically you are saying then, it is a physically conditioned effect?

The Echo: Indeed. Of that of which we speak here, of that of the physical illness.

Director: There are some people who have alcoholism, but don't have this physically conditioned effect. Is that also true?

The Echo: Indeed so. It be here that of the emotionally conditioned.

Director: OK. What exactly does alcohol do to the body when one becomes a full-fledged alcoholic?

The Echo:

Indeed. "Full-fledged" here: The entity be in deservement of an medal. Understand: This be not an easy path. An entity that has attainment of the full-fledged alcoholism, understand, has worked rather hard to attain this state.

Understand: There be here that of the loss of the nutritional values to the body. There be created aggravations to that of the stomach, that of the liver, that of the colon. These be in continuance, resulting in ulcerations of these organs. That of the liver become that refer ossified, solidified, no longer operational. There then be starving of the body, as it were, leaching of the minerals required by the body from the bone structure and a general weakening of the body. That of the blood stream lose its ability of the fighting of infections, as there be here the killing of the white cells. The entity may then find difficulty in that of the quashing of the injuries, difficulties in that of the loss of the spinal fluids and this cause degeneration of the spine, encrustment and dissolvement of the disks of the spine. Also here, there be that of the development of that refer rickets in the area of the lower legs and somewhat of the lower back. However, understand: This be not the case of each and every entity refer alcoholic. It be that of the advance degree of which we speak. There be also here loss of motor controls and indeed loss of thought processes generally.

Director:
Why is it then, that they often reject food, if they are starving?

The Echo: Indeed. Understand: That of the alcohol ingested to that of stomach area, intestinal tract, kill that of the desire of the food, kill that of reference, hunger pangs. Rather, it build desire of further ingestion of the fluid.

Director:

Sounds like they must be in a great deal of pain. Does the alcohol relieve the pain?

The Echo: Momentarily.

Director: Echo, are moderate amounts of alcohol beneficial for the human system?

The Echo: Indeed. Of that here reference, entities of non-resonance of alcoholism, moderate amounts of that refer wines, beers, slight amounts of liquors will do no injuries and indeed be somewhat beneficial in that there be here stimulation of the activities of the body. However, as with anything, over-indulgence be dangerous.

Director: I have heard that wine and bread together are supposed to be beneficial for the brain. Is this true?

The Echo: Indeed. Be somewhat of beneficial. However here, do not use in that of the format of medicinals.

Director: Echo, you mentioned that people who resonate with alcoholism are emotionally unable to cope with the desire for sugar. Is there some way to make them more able to cope, so that they could avoid the alcohol?

The Echo: Indeed Firstly here, of these, entity: removal of the alcohol entirely, removal of the sugars entirely, addition to diet of calciums in high quantities, of lecithins, of vitamin E, vitamin A, vitamin D, and B multiples. Then there be that of the removal also of the salt, of the caffeine, of the red meats: These entity then fare well, if it be so desired.

Director: How would they best cope, or be aided to cope with the withdrawal symptoms?

The Echo: Indeed. Here it be that the of the high amounts of the vitamins E, of the calciums, and of the steady ..... correction .... of the nearly steady inflow of the teas. These be teas of the herbal natures, rather than that refer commercial.

Director: Echo, I have been told by an alcoholic, that there is a continual desire for alcohol, even after many years of abstinence. Is there a reason for that? Can it be overcome?

The Echo: Indeed. Here it be that of the training of the mind, that of the development, within the entity, of the understanding that it, it alone, be in control of its being. Here then, the entity learn that of the methods of mind techniques, as it were, of the removal of the desire. This be an matter of simplicity.

Director: I was also told that an alcoholic has to hit bottom before he will make the effort to overcome this. Is it possible to overcome the damage that has been done to his system physically?

The Echo: Indeed, somewhat. However, as with the punishment of the body, it indeed be physical and indeed there be some effects. However, an entity may minimize these through care of the diet and rest, if it desire. Understand: It indeed be not necessary of an alcoholic be hitting bottom, as it were. Understand: This be observed as that of a turning point of these individuals and more often than not the individual create for its being a thought pattern that dictate to it, that it must follow entire route to near destruction before it may then give self permission to begin return road.

Director: In reference to the nutritional programs you mentioned earlier, would it be necessary for a person to stay on this permanently?

The Echo· Indeed so. Those that be in physical resonance.

Director: There couldn't be a time when they could change their pattern, even slightly?

The Echo: Indeed. Understand: Those in physical resonance have little of real control as the body get, reference, out of hand. Those in mental, psychological resonance may then learn control and after at will.

Director: Are there any genetic factors related to alcoholism, that are passed down?

The Echo: Indeed. Somewhat, of occasion. However, it be more often that of the dealing in that of reference, reincarnational experience. The entity here, example, have existed that of approximate year, 1500, be in format of landowner or landlord, as it were, and be of high degree negativity toward others, in effect, be that of a robber and create difficulty for others that fall within its realm. The entity in a reincarnational experience of the present may have set forth, for its being, a format of punishment in relation to the previous carnation. Understand: It then accept that format for its physical being, refer, alcoholism, just as some entity accept that refer cancer.

Director: Is alcoholism liable to be chosen more than once in physical lives, or is it usually just a one-shot deal?

The Echo: Indeed. Understand: There be no hard fast rules. It be rather, that of the choice of the individual spiritual entity and indeed, may be chose time and time again, if the entity desire that format of reference, repetitive punishment.

Director: Some alcoholics say they are being pushed into drinking by spirits. Does this have some relationship to this decision, made before they are born, to become an alcoholic?

The Echo: Indeed so. Understand here: Rather than that of the pushed, as it were, the entity, in reality, be pushing self. However, in that of the subconscious memory of the entity, there be that of the flash recurrences, flash remembrances of the entity self in past and in spiritual form.
This then be observed by these entity as another or other beings as indeed forcing the entity, cajoling, pushing the entity to continue on this path. In the development of the understanding of this, the entity may then regain control of self, as it were, and follow then which path it do desire.

Director: Is there such a thing then as possession of an alcoholic, or an alcoholic being possessed?

The Echo: Indeed. Understand however: This be that of the format of full permission of the physical entity involved.

Director: Does this account for the personality change that alcoholics develop?

The Echo: Indeed. Somewhat.

Director: They frequently are unable to recall these experiences. Is this just a side effect of the drinking bout itself, or is possession involved here?

The Echo: Understand: There be that of both. Understand also: That of the exorcism here, ritual exorcism, will not here assist, unless the physical entity be emotionally triggered to resist. Understand: Those in involvement of the spiritual realm have no control whatever without that of the totality of agreement of the physical being.

Director: How would one best deal with this situation, possession situation?

The Echo: Indeed. As previous stated: Trigger that of the physical conscious, mind of the physical entity to resist, as it were, expel the entity.

Director: That leads us to hallucinations, delirium tremors, that alcoholics ....

The Echo: Understand: This be that of the physical reactions, responses to that of the difficulty, physical, within the body, within the brain. It be that of a destruction of brain cells. This create the hallucinatory reactions and also that of the tremor response of the body. As previous stated, loss of motor control of the being. Also here, there be involvement of that of physical pain throughout the muscular structure of the being, as there be here also oxygen starvation.

Director: Are any of the things they see real?

The Echo: Indeed. In that of relation of alcohol it be entirety of reality to that of the entity involved, as that refer hallucination, be the entry to that of parallel plane of existence, without the understanding of the plane.

Director: Some of them claim to see strange looking creatures and so on, others, lots of spiders or pink elephants. So some of these beings, then, are actually real?

The Echo: Indeed so. Within that of the existence of the parallel plane.

Director: Please expand a bit on this parallel plane for further understanding.

The Echo: Indeed. It be much as that of the concept God. When an entity have that refer religious experience, it see the form of Christ, the form of God, or that of the angelic hosts before it. This be the observance of that of the parallel plane of existence. In that of the alcoholic hallucinatory state, there be here that of the viewing of the alternate plane. However, the entity be non-selective, have not the capability of selectivity.
In reference here of the plane: Should an entity view within its mind that of the network, a lined grid network, the three dimensional, about, through, around, the entire universe, planet Earth, physical beings, it then have some concept of that of the parallel planes.

Director: This should be easy to understand for people who have solved Rubik's cube.

The Echo: Indeed. Those within computer technology.

Director: Echo, at this time, can you tell me what level the form of Clifford is at, please?

The Echo: Indeed. The form of the one Clifford, trance state K, level 6422 maintained.

Director: Thank You. We talked a lot about the person who is alcoholic themselves. I would like to go on to the coping of the individuals immediately surrounding the person who is the alcoholic. For example, family and friends. What advice can you give them?

The Echo: Indeed. These entity be advised in association of the illness here. They be aware that this indeed be an illness of the physical and/or emotional being. That of the careful considerations of the entity, and without that of the overdoing here, behooves thee.

It be that an entity in involvement of alcoholism will lie and distort. The entities dealing with this in a manner of the family association be aware of this and be in non-acceptance of this, without anger, without emotional heavy, as it were, upon the victim here. That of the careful watching of the entity and that of the understanding of the traumas that the entity be undergoing.

Understand: There be here also emotional, mental, trauma of those associated. These entity have the needs of the development of the understanding, removal of judgmentalism, and that of the development of service to another. In that of format service, it be as these entities be developing in assistance to that refer alcoholic.

However here: Care be exercised in the judging that that which the entity be doing, be wrong. There be this in understanding?

Director: Yes, very much so. I would also ask in conjunction with that: Those of close association to alcoholics would ask the question: "Why me?" What would be the spiritual reason why they would choose to be close to the alcoholic?

The Echo: Indeed. As previous stated: It be that these entity be in requirement of the learning of service to another. In that of the reincarnational understanding here: These entity may have experience alcoholism in that of a previous incarnation and be now viewing that format "from the other side", as it were, and developing the understanding of the other side of alcoholism. These entity also may have be in the format of royalties, lordships, ladies of leisure, or such and have the scorn of their fellow man and accept services lavished upon selves. In present carnation, in dealing of the family member of the alcoholic format, these entity then learning the service format, and in reality be advancing spiritually, rapidly.

Director: Frequently alcoholics are violent. Is it necessary then, that they submit themselves to beatings and so on?

The Echo: Indeed. Understand here: we have not say here, that an entity must remain in association. An entity have entire free choice in its association, and go with the understanding that there be those that have no room within your environment, within your development. However, this format be decided individually, each entity of its own being.

Director: Frequently, people experience a lot of guilt when they contemplate leaving another person, who.........

The Echo: Indeed so. Understand here: That of the guilt here in association of leaving another or not performing for another in reality be that of the acceptance of social doctrines of the past and the guilt be self-inflicted, as guilt may never be inflicted by another. It may be suggested by another, but the individual must inflict guilt upon self. And we here then ask you: WHY?

Director: What about the alcoholic himself? How does guilt affect him?

The Echo: Indeed. Here be somewhat similar of that previous spake. There be here that the alcoholic find its being socially unacceptable, its acts be of occasion socially unacceptable. Therefore, the entity hide its being in alcohol, and this be that of the vicious circle. The entity then emotionally, mentally, punish its being as well and continue faster, more frenzied, in its self-destruct path.

Director: Are there any specific blockages in the chakras, that would create a tendency towards alcoholism?

The Echo: Indeed. Of individuals here, there may be that of the crown chakra, throat chakra, base chakra, either or, but individual.

Director: How can these blockages be removed?

The Echo: Indeed. Understand here: There be no necessity of removal. The question be asked with an assumption that alcoholism be "bad". Understand here: It be an individual decision. That of the alcoholism indeed be destructive. However, the judgment of the good or bad here lie within the individual, as there be a relationship to that of possible reincarnational causes here.

Director: Right. One of the better known organizations to aid alcoholism, as one of their primary steps, the alcoholic has to keep saying and admitting publicly to himself and his friends:

"I am an alcoholic", saying over and over again. Do you agree this is a good method?

The Echo: Indeed not. With the supposition that these entity require curing, this indeed be not a method of affecting cure. This be rather affirmation of continuance.

Understand: the triggering here be better stated such as: "I am normal". "I am the same, similar to others". Remove that of the term "alcoholic", and that of the curing process be affected simply and rapidly.

Director: They say that a person must acknowledge that he is an alcoholic before he can.....................

The Echo: Indeed so. Understand: The entity need not acknowledge each and every minute of each and every day, as that of the realization in the conscious mind, that the entity say indeed it be alcoholic, be a major breakthrough. Here this be enough.

That of the repeating merely fortify alcoholism.

Director: What additional insights and advice could you give to those people who run these types of organizations, so that they may aid the alcoholics further?

The Echo: Indeed. Firstly here: There be that format of the standing to testify. An entity then look out upon its peers and say "I am an alcoholic. This is my story". Rather here; we of the Echo would suggest that of "Alcoholics Anonymous" be a misnomer, in that of an entity saying "I am an alcoholic", it no longer be anonymous. Therefore we say here, that of the gathering indeed of those that be claimed alcoholic and these entity be assisted in that of the format of self-esteem program and then that of the standing before the peers to say "I am an alcoholic" will come naturally.

Director: Alcoholics will often use the excuse of their helplessness to keep other people serving them. How helpless are they?

The Echo: Indeed, Not. Understand here: We of the Echo do not here assume sympathy of these entity, as these entity be highly capable in their own right. It merely be needs that those about the entity be in non-acceptance of manipulation, as previous stated.

Director: Rather than sympathy, then compassion?

The Echo: Indeed.

Director:
Is there anything you would like to say before closing? I see our time is just about up here.

The Echo:
Indeed. Here, we say: that of the form of the one Clifford have be in close resonance of that refer "alcoholic:. The entity here maintain little or no sympathy of the entity alcoholic and oft times, the form of the one Clifford be judged brutal, unfeeling. However, here understand: We of the Echo say here: this entity have the tendency of the following that which it see fit of a second in time, and here we say: It have perform admirably.
Indeed. Understand: Of occasion we must boost that of our sleeping friend.

Director:
That's beautiful.

The Echo: Form of the one Clifford become somewhat of rigidity. We must at this point, release the form.

Director: Thank you for this session.

The Echo: Indeed. We of the Echo, thank thee of the opportunity of approach. Therefore, we say to you:

Go in peace. Go in love and understanding.

Chapter 12   The Mitchell-Hedges Crystal Skull
Part 1

Martindale Road St. Catharines, Ontario   February 17, 1996
10:15 p.m

This session was performed in the presence of the Mitchell-Hedges Crystal Skull. This life-sized skull is made of pure stone quartz crystal and is a perfect replica of a human head. The teeth are perfect and the jaw is removable and hinged. The entire artifact consists of one single rock crystal, a world treasure and a world mystery.

Anna "Sammy" Mitchell-Hedges was present to offer a presentation about the skull. Twenty-four other persons were present.

Director:	Is all well with the form Clifford?
The Echo:	Indeed. The form of the one Clifford, trance state H, level 543, broadening naturally.
Director:	Thank You. Echo, this session is going to be fairly short. It is going to be on the crystal skull. There will be four people who will be asking questions. OK. First of all will you locate Bob, please.
Bob:	Hello Echo.

The Echo:	Indeed. Form found .... Greetings
Bob:	Um.. the question, or two small questions, sort of related:.. the crystal skull, does it belong to the Mayans when it was carved out? and how many life-times did it take to produce one skull?
The Echo:	That of the original belonging, indeed be not that here referred Mayan. This be that which be referred here Atlantean, and this be here referred created rather than that refer carved, and in the time duration, the requirement of the process of creation be that of approximate forty-eight hours. Understand that of the creation be performed through that here refer concentration format of the individuals in knowledge of crystalline structures. Individuals numbering twelve and these entity indeed concentrate in unison and create that which be before thee of their concentration format.
Director:	You said it took them 48 hours to make. Is that what you said? With 12 people?
The Echo:	Indeed so.
Director:	How many years ago was that?
The Echo:	In your terms of years, that of approximate here, 100,000.
Director:	I've had different impressions here. When I touched that thing, I went outside the earth.
The Echo:	Indeed so.

215

Director:	Well, can you explain that? (side comment from someone... They didn't say where it was made...) Where was it made, then?
The Echo:	Indeed. Within that here refer the realm of that presently refer Sirius.
Director:	OK. So will you comment on why I was seeing outside of the Earth? Please?
The Echo:	Indeed. That be of construction of that here refer realm Sirius.
Director:	Oh, That's another planet? OK ! Good! And that was 100,000 years ago?
The Echo:	Indeed, that be that refer estimation.
Director:	Thank you
Bob:	Thank you.
Director:	So when I touched that skull, then I was right about what I was getting?
The Echo:	Indeed so. Do the entity ever err?
Director:	(laughing) Sometimes I wonder. more laughter) To Bob- Did that answer all your questions?
Bob:	Yes, Thank You, you answered
The Echo:	Indeed so.
Director:	You answered mine too. I appreciate that. Thank you.

The Echo:	Indeed. That here refer director, be of high degree deviousness. (Linda's laughter)
Director:	I love you too. (laughingly)
The Echo:	Indeed so. (Group laughter, including Linda)
Director:	OK ... Lynn
LYNN:	Greetings Echo. And by the way, thank you, because that was a question I would liked to have asked as well. I'm more interested at this moment ... because this gentle lady (Sammy) has received the care of this magnificent gift, I was wondering if she has been in past lifetimes, connected to the skull and how many in this room have also had a connection to the skull.
The Echo:	Indeed. That of the form Anna, indeed so. Do understand this entity be here refer member that refer priestly organization of that refer the land Atlantis. Understand here, that refer Atlantis be of the entire planet of that refer Earth, and that of the major locations of the here energy forces be located that of the area presently refer central Atlantic ocean, that refer Central America, and that refer here lower China. These be the highest concentration of population areas. The entity present be in earthly form and be in charge, as it were, of crystal energies and that refer the skull be a portion of its charge.
Lynn:	Is there anyone else in the room who has also been connected with the skull?
The Echo:	Indeed. There be that here of all present.

217

Lynn:	We're all here by special invitation because we all are connected to it?
The Echo:	Indeed so. Through that here refer various points in that refer time.
Director: Echo?	Would you like to talk a little bit more on that,

The Echo: Indeed. Merely to say that throughout that time span here refer 100,000 years, the entities present be in contact of this communication device at one point in time or another. Beyond that, specifics be in requirement of deeper investigations.

Lynn:	Is it possible, of the 12 that helped create it, are any of them alive today, amongst us?
The Echo:	Reference "amongst us"
Director:	The ones in this group.
The Echo:	Indeed not of the present.
Lynn:	Is this why I'm picking up so much alien in the skull, because I'm seeing their original form?
The Echo:	Indeed so.
Lynn:	Thank You.
Director:	Boy, that's putting a lot of questions in my head (laughter) OK. Mimi..
Mimi:	Echo, why have we been all called together tonight, by the skull? What's the purpose?

The Echo:	Indeed. Understand, there be that of an growing understanding, an growing enlightening, as it were. Those present be that here refer forerunners of this format. That of the communication energies of that here refer the crystal skull do draw to it those that may go forth and assist that here loosely refer mankind. In the using, directing, receiving the energies of the communicating device, the entities may then further assist their fellow man.
Director:	Boy, this is putting a lot of questions in me, but, I'll have to save them for another time ....Marilyn?
Marilyn:	Good evening, Echo, I'd just like to ask .... the other skulls that exist on the earth, how are they connected to this one, and is this one the original and the other ones, like a copy, or how are they connected?
The Echo:	Indeed. That of the present format be of seven in number. These be here refer, scattered presently about the planet Earth. That of the reference other skulls, replicas be indeed produced in similar manner and be here refer lesser devices of communication. Do understand, in the use of that here refer harmonic sounds, this device may then communicate with all others at once and the same time. An entity must needs only to find that of here refer the correct frequency pattern and the crystal skulls about the planet will all emanate the same energy as the one to which the harmonics be applied.
Director:	Echo, the first time I saw the skull, I saw the aura about twenty feet outside the house.

219

The Echo:	Indeed so. It be that refer here protective aura. Do understand. This may not be removed by an entity that be not in resonance with it.
Director:	So even though Sammy's not there, that energy to protect her is always with her?
The Echo:	Indeed so.
Director:	That's good.
The Echo:	Understand, this entity present have indeed experienced an life pattern in present that do indeed include an high degree of risk factors. The entity understand that it have attained to present relatively unscathed and this be due to that here refer the protective aura of the crystal skull and that of the divine purpose of the entity present.
Director:	Is that because she has the love around her all the time? Because I've always felt that this skull only... has the love in it and training and healing, so is it the love... (Echo interrupted)
The Echo:	Indeed so. Do understand, the energy be there to be used in a loving, positive, helpful manner. Do this device be in attempt of use in that here refer negative or evil manner, the entity so attempting will be immediately affected by its own avarices.
Director:	Terrific. So the skull is reflecting its negativity?
The Echo:	Indeed so.
Director:	Great.

The Echo:	Correction. Rather than reflecting, the term in your language be rejecting.
Director:	Terrific. (Whisper ... Mary suggests Sammy ask a question) Sammy, do you have a question?
Sammy :	Am I going to make this expedition?
The Echo:	Indeed. The entity will find the opportunity of travel here the approximate ending of the month here refer July of the present year. The entity indeed will travel and will indeed find it standing upon its prior temple of existence.
Sammy:	Thank You.
The Echo:	Understand, in the traveling, of that of the protection of the crystal skull, we of the Echo also send to thee an portion of we, in order that thee be further protected and that the travel be of entire safety.
Director:	Looks like you have part of the The Echo with you always now.
	Is there anything you would like to say, Echo, before we close this session?
The Echo:	We would, at a time further, in that refer future, proceed further within questioning format of such. Here we would suggest that of here the meetings at the home of the form of the one Clifford and the form of the one Linda. Suggestion here be that here refer Monday next.

Director:	OK. Next Monday then. There will be no charge for that .... except your two dollars when you come in. (Jokingly) <center>(Group laughter)</center>
The Echo:	At this time we would then release the form.
Director:	Thank you for this session, Echo.
The Echo:	Indeed. We of the Echo, thank thee of the opportunity of approach, therefore we say to thee...Go in peace. Go in love and understanding.
	Follow an way such as the Nazarene .

Session ended at 10:35 P.M.

Upon waking, Cliff had an impression of a stone tower that had a recessed flat top in which about ten or twelve persons were sitting and seemed to be meditating. He said the tower was very high and had a mysterious aura about it.

Linda and the group felt that this was how the crystal skull was made.

Chapter 13   The Mitchell-Hedges Crystal Skull
Part 2

February, 1996

Director: Marilyn has no question. How about you Terry?

Terry: Sure.

Director: OK. Go ahead

Terry: Hi Echo, its Terry. What is the purpose of the skulls?

The Echo: Indeed. As prior stated, that here refer crystalline skulls, be that of communication devices. These be created in the form of that refer the human skull, in order to impress the users with that of the understandings and the knowledges contained therein. Do understand: The knowledges that be within the skull, be merely that refer skull, be an magnification device that be used in communication techniques. That of the skull be approached with that refer harmonic resonance at an frequency ... correction.. at an particular frequency and all other here refer skulls about the planet will resonate at the same frequency at once and the same time.

Director: Are you saying that when someone channels through the skull, that it is actually going through seven of them?

The Echo: Indeed not.

Director: Oh, I misunderstood.

The Echo: Rather than that term channel, we do say, that of the use here of that refer harmonic sound frequencies.

Director: Oh, so .... helping one, then it is going through all seven?

The Echo: Indeed. Through that of the seven, indeed so. Also all others that be somewhat similarly constructed.

Terry: So communication is between, say myself and the skull, or the skull and some other foreign party?

The Echo: Indeed not. Understand. In the creation of an device that with emanate an particular sound, here further refer an black box, do this black box be brought close to an crystal skull and its frequency directed to the skull, all other skulls about the entire planet will then receive this harmonic sound frequency and will vibrate and send out the frequency at once and the same time. In this manner the frequency may be changed deliberately at specific points in time and in this manner an communication signal can then be sent forth. Indeed, from any one skull to any and all of other skulls.

Terry: And where do they receive their information?

The Echo: Indeed. Reference they.

Terry: The skulls. Where is their information drawn from?

The Echo:	Indeed. Exterior applications from here refer human individual. Understand, in your time and understanding there be that here refer Morse code. An entity may be at one particular point of the planet and in the use of the Morse code, may send an message to another point of the planet, to an here refer similar device. This device may then receive the message and repeat the message in audible terms. Do thee understand? This be that of which refer skulls usage. An entity using an harmonic generator close to any of the skulls, may then send an message of sound, interruption, sound, interruption, sound, interruption. This will be then received and repeated by all other like devices.
Director:	We better move around. Do you have a question? No? OK, next.
Lois:	OK Echo, its Lois. So are you saying its used as a communication device around the planet Earth, or is it being used as communication between other planets?
The Echo:	Indeed. That of original use be among that here refer many planets.
Director:	Many planets?
The Echo:	That refer many planets.
Director:	Would you please comment on that. Tell us a little bit about that?
The Echo:	Indeed, as prior stated, the building of the device, in the replication of that refer human skull, be that of the retention of knowledges, informations etc. That this device contain, or may be used to transmit knowledges, informations etc. and this

be placed severally upon a number of here refer habitable, planets and the emanations may be then easily transmitted to any location of any that refer distance.

Director: Are you saying that these planets then are putting their energy, their questions, their assistance, to these other skulls on this planet? Is that what you are saying? They are directing from other planets?

The Echo: Indeed. That here refer were. It be that refer past tense.

Director: So they're not doing it now.

The Echo: Indeed not.

Director: What planets were they?

The Echo: Indeed. These be that beyond refer here solar system.

Director: Are those names available to us?

The Echo: Indeed not of present.

Director: Is there a reason for that?

The Echo: Indeed. It be that of the deviousness (loud group laughter) of the one director. Understand, these information, be that refer a degree lost in that refer time.

Director: You did mention Sirius. Are there others? How many others are then doing this?

226

The Echo: Indeed. Reference others.

Director: Well, how many. Were there seven planets, or more than that, that you were mentioning?

The Echo: Indeed. Of that of the drawing informations here, there be that of approximate 40.

Director: Oh wow! Should we do another session on that one Echo? (group laughter)

The Echo: Indeed. As you wish.

Director: Do you have a question?

Fran: Hi Echo, its Fran. Is the crystal skull being used for any purpose on Earth right now?

The Echo: Indeed so. That of the here refer crystal skull, that which be retained by that of Anna Mitchell-Hedges, this indeed be used an great deal by many, throughout the world to indeed magnify that of the mental energies directed to it for the purpose of healings, as healing assistances.

Director: OK. I wasn't really understanding what that was all about.

The Echo: Indeed. Understand, here refer many entity in awareness of the Mitchell-Hedges skull. In their meditative states, focus their mental energies upon the skull and use the skull to magnify these energies in order to assist others that may be in requirement of the healing formats.

Director: Like we have done a couple of times?

227

The Echo:	Indeed so.
Director:	OK.
Chris:	Well, I did have a question, but its been answered. Thank you. I will ask another one right now, Echo, Thank you. I was going to ask if, but, it has been answered in a way, I was going to ask, was the crystal skull did it come by accident to this planet or was there an intent or purpose, but you have already answered that.
The Echo:	Indeed. That it indeed be that refer brought into reality with purpose. It do not be brought to the planet. It be created upon the planet yet it be created here refer mentally.
Chris:	I see. Thank you.
Director:	The way we were asking on Saturday, because when I had seen that it came from another planet, your saying that people from another planet created it from another planet, but it was created here on this planet. Is that what you are saying?
The Echo:	Indeed so,
Director:	Oh. That's interesting
Chris:	Yes, that was interesting. Thank you Echo.
Lynn:	Echo, greetings, um, when I looked into the skull, I saw many, many pictures, of course, but the one that really has me questioning, is why did I see so many children, young children in it. What was the skull trying to relate?

228

The Echo:	Indeed. Understand, within that of here refer the culture of the Mayan peoples, the descendants of that here refer Atlanteans, these entity develop a religious understanding that include the use of the skulls crystals in an degree here refer negative mind. These entity tend to present the skull as the symbolization of an religious deity. In this manner the crystal skulls oft-time oversee that of the sacrifice of human life in here comparative terms, most often this deal of children prior the age of that refer twelve years of development.

Lynn:	Was I one of those children?
The Echo:	Indeed so. Of occasion.
Lynn:	More than once?
The Echo:	Indeed so.
Lynn:	Thank you.
Director:	Debbie?

Debbie:	Hi Echo, it is Debbie, um....

The Echo:	It is indeed.

(group laughter)

Debbie:	(Laughing) Now I'm thrown off ... With the indulgence of every one here, my question is a little more personal. When I was in the energy circle that night with the skull, I was given a message regarding.. to focus on a four leaf clover. I was wondering if the Echo could possibly give me any more information, as I have yet to come with anything other than St. Patrick's day.

(Side comment ... Green beer?)

The Echo:	Indeed. Understand that of the four-leaf clover be that of an representation to the entity. That of

the message here be rather that of the focus, the meditation upon that of the balancing of the four aspects of self. This be that of the mental, emotional, spiritual and physical balance. The entity in its meditation here focus upon all four equally to assist its being further.

Director: Does it have anything to do with the skull, because   she .....

The Echo: Indeed. Not in particular of the skull. Merely that it be an magnification of the intensity of the presentation.

Director: The skull then is not sending any energy towards
her?

The Echo: Indeed so.

Director: Oh, It was

The Echo: As it is stated, it be indeed in magnification of the presentation of the entities thought processes.

Director: OK. So it had to do with that.

Debbie.   Thank you very much, Echo.

Director: OK Michael.

Michael: Hi Echo. I'd like to-after the session on Saturday night, I had an image from a dream. I'd like to say I think it might be a message for somebody. What I saw in this image, was Cliff Preston, there at the site, or in the vicinity, or something and he was writing on a rock on the ground,   with   chalk   or something ... along long long name, maybe thirty or forty letters in it and then we had to clear off a bit of the leaves and dirt and write this name and it was the name of a tree and the idea was that wherever these trees grew in abundance, that's where they would find more of these ruins. I knew that Anna would be going down there so I was just wondering if there was some sort of message associated for somebody, so I thought I should say it.

The Echo: Indeed. We be drawn, in the searching here to that refer colparolmaylaleenapol. This sound in even our knowledges be an highly localized name for a tree of which there be long and narrow serrated edged leaves. These leaves and branches be of high degree sharpness and in the areas of this growth patterns indeed there be the findings of which they search. These trees grow in these areas because of high intensity of that mineral here refer zinc, as this be used an great deal within that refer the utensils of the people here refer Mayan.

Director: Did this have anything to do with the skull?

The Echo: Indeed not. However, this may be used as an indication of direction and location for that here refer the party of that refer Mitchell-Hedges expedition.

Michael: Did this have to do .... I had the impression it had to with their search for the crystal..um .. mines, perhaps.

The Echo: Indeed. Understand, hat of the zinc here will draw them indeed closer.

Michael: What was the name of that tree, again?

The Echo: portion....	Colparolmanu ..... We have lost the last
	(group laughter)
	We would advise the entities that they listen closely to the taping devic e.
Director:	We'll listen to the tape. Rena.....You pass? OK Arden? No questions? Well, David does.
DAVID:	Oh yeah, You betcha. I've been absolute..oh.. Good evening Echo, I'm sorry .....
The Echo:	Indeed. We are not sorry. It is indeed a good evening. (group laughter)
DAVID:	I have been completely fascinated with this since I held the skull myself, and talked with Anna Mitchell-Hedges and I've been piecing together little bits and pieces of information that I got from Saturday night, from the book and from various other places, and I was wondering ...A hundred thousand years ago, when the skull was made, I was thinking that the volume of water on the plane would have been more.. a lot more than it is now, and I was wondering, if one, the harmonic form of communication with the skull had any thing to do with the dolphins and the whales and elephants, and I was also wandering if the Atlantean people at that time were amphibious, or had amphibious capabilities, like harmonic communication.

232

The Echo:	Indeed. EH Ӊ What did he say? (group laughter)
	Indeed. To the form of the one David, We jest with thee.
	Do understand. That refer here whales, that refer dolphins, that refer elephants of these three there be one that be native to the land-correction-to the planet Earth. That refer elephant be native. That refer whale, that refer dolphin, that refer ostrich and that refer platypus be indeed brought to the planet and be the results of that refer here genetic experimentations that be evolved beyond that here refer one hundred thousand years in time, in time as you know. Atlantean humans indeed maintain an degree of that here refer amphibious abilities. However, it be not that refer gills. Rather it be that of the control of the mind over the body to that point that the breathing process may be halted or interrupted for an desired length of time.
Director:	Would you help Lynn, please Echo?
The Echo:	Indeed. Understand. The form Lynn be in allowance here of an characterization degree change. We do say to this entity, that at this point of time, it be not in proper approach. Therefore, we would say to this entity that it withdraw at this point of time and the form of the one Lynn be returned to full control of this entity, now.
Wilma:	Hi Echo, its Wilma. You have mentioned Atlantis.... Are our scientists ever

233

going to acknowledge that there was an Atlantis, and is our scientific society going to ever come to that understanding?

The Echo: Indeed. Do understand those entity that spend an lifetime in that refer here an structured learning process. Learn in reality to be blind to other than that which they have been taught. Therefore here do understand. That refer scientific community be almost entirely unaware of the two hundred prior earthly civilizations rises and falls. Rather, they prefer to believe, in their personal conceit, that of the present civilization be that refer one and only.

Director: What level is the form of Cliff in now Echo?

The Echo: Indeed. That of the form of the one Clifford, trance state M, level four-one-nine maintain.

Director: Will he go, yet, deeper than that even?

The Echo: Indeed. To an period of time, in time as you know, of approximate two minute duration to that level refer here Q.

Director: I'm having a hard time with what people are saying. I guess I'm going to have to...

The Echo: Indeed. We will then here offer the surrounding of that refer insulating protection

Director: Thank you. Next ....No? .... How about you? Do you have a question?

LINDA: Hi Echo, this is Linda. I'd like to know if energy directed towards the Mitchell-Hedges skull, will touch the one that's in England.

234

The Echo:	Indeed. Reference one in England.
LINDA:	The one that's in the museum in London.
The Echo:	Indeed so. Do understand, however, there be one difficulty in this format. That of the British skull be ensconced beneath that refer glass and there be within this glass that here refer lead composition and this will then create an barrier to the communication of this skull. This will also allow of this refer British skull, gradual decomposition to occur.
LINDA:	Is there some way that one could get through the lead so that ... to help the skull so that it doesn't decompose?
The Echo:	Indeed. That of the use of that here refer hammer.
	(loud laughter from the group)
Director:	Were you joking, Echo?
The Echo:	Indeed not. That here refer an living crystal must needs that of contact with the oxygen, argon, and all of the other elements of the atmosphere in order for it to maintain its living qualities.
Director:	Echo, you mentioned once before that there are seven skulls, original ones. Can you say where they are, and how they can be found?
The Echo:	Indeed. There be that of the location here refer Central Prairies, plains of North America. Buried here at a proximate depth of two hundred fifty feet. This be the resultant of the receding of the seas and the subsequent siltation over the years. Be that of the here refer Nazca plain and adjoining mountains to the Nazca plain and there be here the

third skull at the base of that here refer alabaster tunnels. There be that refer the Rift valley of Africa. Within caves here, at the base of that refer Rift escarpment. There be that of refer Xanadu valley in China among the archeology diggings presently there, they be of extreme proximity.

Director: Echo, you mentioned that they couldn't do what they were supposed to do, if they were buried or covered.....

The Echo: Indeed so.

Director: So,   if   they're   found...until they're found then the others can't be used completely. Is that so?

The Echo: Indeed so.

(Side comment. . ."There is still two more. Still two more.")

Director: Is there still two more?

The Echo: Indeed. Within that here refer Ural mountains caves here at an depth of approximate 1,400 feet. That here refer Lake Superior at depths thereof.
Director: What are the chances of discovering these, finally?

The Echo: At the present observation, China, Africa, approximately 50 percent, that of the Ural mountains, approximately 10 percent, that of Lake Superior, that of here approximate 60 percent.

Director: Sixty?

The Echo: That of refer Central Plains, approximate two percent.

Director:	How then can they be found? And who would be finding them?
The Echo:	Indeed. Present viewing, highest probability be accidental discovery.
Director:	Is there anybody in this group or anybody that we know who may locate one of them?
The Echo:	Indeed. Not of present resonance.
Chuna:	Hi Echo, my name is Chuna. I'd like to know if there is any correlation between the ascension that is talked about in the book... the "Crystal Stair", if there is any connection there?
The Echo:	Indeed. There be not indeed. Understand that refer "Ascension" be that of an metaphor for that refer the enlightenment of the human minds and that of that refer the crystal skull, may indeed also assist of this format, however this be not of its primary or only purpose.
Director:	Mary?
Mary:	Hi Echo. It's Mary. I just want to know what the purpose of me viewing the skull was. It was sort of a special invitation which Lynn asked about, and I'm wondering.
The Echo:	Indeed. Do understand, of this entity. This entity be aware of the numerology accompanying self be identical to that of the numerology accompanying that here refer Sri Sathya Sai Baba. This entity be in that, here refer, divine purpose of present existence. That of the viewing be an primary step to its enlightenment format.
Mary:	Thank You Echo.
The Echo:	Indeed not. We Thank Thee.

237

(Laughter)

Mary: I love your sense of humor. (Laughter)

Director: I do too. Does any one else have a question?

Wilma: I'd like to ask a general question. Echo, it's Wilma, I'm wondering why the skull has been brought to our attention at this time. Is that a positive sign for us?

The Echo: Indeed so. Understand. This particular grouping, as prior stated, be in resonance in association of this communication device refer, skull, of numerous prior incarnations. Of the present thee be drawn to approach the skull once more in order of the expanding, or here refer the opening of the mind processes of each entity in contact.

Director: Terry?

Terry: Yes, is it possible for a human to recreate the vibrations that he needs to create to speak to the skull?

The Echo: Indeed so. Understand this may also be an means of locating some of the others.

Terry: Do you have to be in a trance state to do this?

The Echo: Indeed not. The entities may experience with that refer harmonics in order to find the correct resonance.
That of the form of the one Clifford gaining in rigidity. We would then allow that of a two minute duration. We must then release the form.

238

Director:	Echo, is there anything that you would like ... information you would like to give us at this point?
The Echo:	Indeed. Merely that in retention of the knowledge of that here refer the skull, be indeed that of an communication device. The entities may use its energies regardless of proximity. The entities may use this as an magnification device also.
Director:	I'm feeling like Cliff is still going deeper now, so ...I have all kinds of questions now that this is over, but, thank you very much for this session, Echo.
The Echo:	We of The Echo, thank thee, of the opportunity of approach. Therefore we say to thee:

> Go in peace, Go in love and understanding, Follow an way, such as the Nazarene,
> We release the form.

Chapter 14   Code of Living and Other Statements

The Echo's Code of Living presented during a deep-trance channeling session of The Echo by Cliff Preston in 1983. Cliff and Linda Preston have since followed this ethic in their daily lives.

Make every effort to see problems from both your viewpoint and the viewpoint of others.

Harm no one, physically, mentally, emotionally, or spiritually.

Do not cause others to experience guilt or fear.

Do cause others to experience love and trust of you.

Remove judgmentalism from your thought processes.

Remember the Universal Law of Karma: You will reap what you sow.

Offer assistance and understand, if it is turned down, that each entity has total free choice in its life.

The only crime is to force another to any action or thought against its will.

View all beings as spirits and you will begin to see the beauty of them all.

Treat no one in any manner that you could not or would not accept for self.

Those entities that think they can, can.
Those entities that think they can't, are completely correct.
(1980)

Belief is that which you have been taught and have accepted as truth.
Truth is that which you have personally experienced and examined. (1983)

Love is the only answer, regardless the question. (1985)

To blindly follow the belief of another is to accept the totality of mental and emotional slavery. (1987)

Crossing Over:
Please remember, that no one is ever really lost.
Crossing over is just another part of the human experience and for most it is a welcome change. The person is birthing into the Spiritual Realm and someday soon, when it chooses, will birth again into the Physical Realm.
So it continues for each of us until we have finally learned all we feel we need to learn and can then return to our Godhead.
Only those left behind mourn for the lost one, and in fact, the mourning is most often for self, not for the loved one.
Rather than mourn or fret at the passing of your loved one, celebrate that you have associated with her/him and have contributed in some manner, yet unknown to you, to the enrichment of her/his experience.
Send them on with Love and the knowledge that, if you wish, you may meet again, at another time and another place, to continue helping each other in your travels through experience and time. (2002)

Go in peace. Go in love and understanding. (For many years, the final message of The Echo at every deep-trance channeling session by Cliff Preston.)

Help is always available

If you want answers to your questions about life
or help with any problem, large or small,
Cliff and Linda Preston may be able to help.

A channeling session of The Echo can give you answers
about various areas of your life such as
health and medical information, relationships, career and
finances, and dream interpretation.

Hypnosis, tarot card readings, handwriting analysis,
numerology and other disciplines can provide insight into
your life and practical help with such things as stress
management or overcoming negative thinking and
unwanted habits.

Learn to do what Cliff and Linda do

Cliff and Linda offer courses in psychic and spiritual
development such as self-awareness, meditation and
automatic writing; and past-life workshops.

Learn more at   cpreston@becon.org

Order Form

To order copies of
Cliff Preston channels The Echo Book 1
Cliff Preston channels The Echo Book 2
Cliff Preston channels The Echo Book 3

please detach or photocopy this form, print clearly, and
mail it with your cheque payable to

Cliff Preston
79 Burleigh Road North
Ridgeway ON Canada L0S 1N0

Send to:
Name _____

Address _____

_____
Prov/State_____Postal/Zip_____
Country _____
Email _____

Copy(s) at $24.95
       Book 1 _____
       Book 2 _____
       Book 3 _____
       Add delivery $4.00 Canada
                 $5.00 U.S.

     Total Books _____ Total Amount_____